Money Guide
Your Home

By the Editors of *Money*

Andrews, McMeel & Parker

A Universal Press Syndicate Company
Kansas City/New York

For further information write
Andrews, McMeel & Parker,
a Universal Press Syndicate Company,
4900 Main Street, Kansas City, Missouri 64112.

Library of Congress Cataloging-in-Publication Data

Money guide.

1. House buying.   2. House selling.   3. Home
ownership—Costs.   4. Real estate investment.   5. Real estate
business.   I. Money (Chicago, Ill.)
HD1379.M65   1986   643'.1   86-1196
ISBN 0-8362-2209-1

The material in this book was previously published in magazine
format as *Money Guide: Your Home* by
Money magazine, a publication of Time, Inc.

───────ATTENTION: SCHOOLS AND BUSINESSES───────

Andrews, McMeel & Parker books are available at quantity discounts with bulk
purchase for educational, business, or sales promotional use. For information, please
write to: Special Sales Department, Andrews, McMeel & Parker, 4900 Main Street,
Kansas City, Missouri 64112.

Acknowledgments

The editors especially wish to thank the following people for their assistance in preparing the *Money Guide:* Eldon Ewing and Robert Raffanti, Santa Clara Valley Associates/Red Carpet Real Estate, Campbell, California; Michael S. Johnson, professor of economics, University of New Orleans; Cathey Manley, president, Interior Design Society, Chicago; Randall M. Rothstein, attorney, Bethesda, Maryland; Frances Schwartz, manager of credit policy, Citibank, New York City; George Sliker, Green Landing Nursery, Upper Marlboro, Maryland.

Foreword

The purpose of this *Money Guide* is to help you make the biggest financial decisions of your life—the purchase, remodeling, and sale of the house you live in. It will give you the information you need to find a house that will appreciate and the questions you should ask brokers and bankers, architects and contractors, lawyers and landscapers, as well as potential buyers and sellers. The *Guide* will take you through every stage of the home-buying process, from the first time you scout out a neighborhood to the settlement, when you put your signature on the biggest check you've ever written. If you want to fix up a house you own, it will show you the most profitable ways to do it. If you want to invest in residential real estate, it will explain how to make money as a landlord.

This guide was prepared by *Money* staffers, many of whom have stood in your shoes as home buyers and owners. The team was directed by senior editor Julie Connelly and supervised overall by assistant managing editor Frank B. Merrick. Connelly grew up in the New York City suburb of New Rochelle and now lives in Manhattan. She researched her topic by traveling as far as Houston (for the convention of the National Association of Home Builders) and as close to home as Levittown, New York, the prototype suburb that was bulldozed out of Long Island potato fields after World War II and made home ownership an affordable, graspable dream for most Americans. It also gave to the language a name that has become a description of tract housing.

Today's new homes cost more than 10 times as much as the Levittown bungalows, but the dream of home ownership remains as deeply rooted as ever in the national psyche. "I suspect that to everyone a house is synonymous with security," says Connelly. "Have you ever walked down a suburban street at night with the lights on in the windows of all the houses? You can't really see what's going on in those houses, but whatever it is, it looks from outside to be warm, glamorous, safe, and unchanging."

LANDON Y. JONES
Executive Editor, *Money*

Introduction

From colonial times, Americans have preferred their own back-yards to more public places. A fledgling nation civilized a vast frontier in little more than a century by giving land to anyone who would bust the sod and build a log cabin. Ever since, owning a home has been a reward for thrift and industry and a cornerstone of American life.

It still is. In 1985, 42 million Americans were between the ages of 25 and 34, the years when most of us buy our first homes. Fortunately, real gains in income and substantial declines in mortgage rates mean that more of these young people can afford to buy a place than at any time since 1979. Because housing starts have also hit their highest levels in five years, there will be plenty of homes for them to choose from.

The building industry has always been conscious of the first-time buyer's need for low-priced housing. In 1926, Sears, Roebuck sold its Honor-Bilt kit houses for as little as $474, shipping the precut pieces by train from factory to homesites for owners to assemble. In 1942, Frank Lloyd Wright designed two-bedroom $4,000 houses for Detroit auto workers. After World War II, William J. Levitt's Cape Cod-style tract homes, with just 750 square feet of interior space, sold for $6,990.

But the era of cheap housing has vanished along with cheap cars, cheap energy, and cheap ground round. The median price of a new home today is $80,000. As a result, first-time home buyers have to shop diligently to make sure they are getting top value for their dollars. This *Money Guide* will help you be a better housing shopper; it will tell you how to choose a place to live and how to finance it. You will also learn how to improve your home so that when you sell it you can get top dollar. For this is the remarkable thing about a house: there is scarcely another product that you can buy, use, and then sell—for more than you paid for it.

CONTENTS

A Beginner's Choices

Candace E. Trunzo

> Owning a home is not an impossible dream if your expectations are down to earth.

If young Americans have one thing going for them in their search for shelter today, it's choice. There is no denying that prices went through the roof for a decade and that mortgage rates still hover in the teens. But incomes are rising fast enough so that housing today consumes less of the median family intake—28 percent—than it did in 1981 and 1982, when it ate up 36 percent. Moreover, the combination of new types of cost-efficient housing and flexible methods of financing has created more opportunities for young men and women to get a foot in the door of home ownership. The U.S. League of Savings Institutions reports that newcomers now account for 41 percent of annual home sales, up from 13.5 percent in 1981.

Being a homeowner puts a considerable strain on family finances, but most Americans still aspire to living in a single-family detached house with lots of space and a private yard. Unfortunately, higher prices, lower appreciation, and bigger mortgages may prevent you from making this dream come true the first time around. But you need not be fenced out altogether. Your options include condominiums—which have replaced tract houses as the starter homes—existing or new houses, factory-produced dwellings, and homes you can build yourself. By choosing as carefully as did the five buyers described in this chapter, you will be able not only to take pleasure in your home while you live in it, but also to parlay it perhaps into a more substantial spread later on.

CONDOMINIUMS

If you have always yearned to live in a home designed by a well-known architect, you may be able to do so by buying a unit in a condominium development. The challenge of creating attractive, reasonably priced housing for middle-income people has encouraged such specialists as Barry Berkus in Santa Barbara, John Bloodgood in Des Moines, and Victor Mirontschuk in Houston to draw the plans for many of these densely populated, self-contained communities.

Condos can be apartment buildings, attached townhouses, or clusters of detached houses in the heart of downtown or out in the suburbs. Each owner has title to his own living space and shares possession of such common areas as lawns, swimming pools, and tennis courts. Buyers have all the advantages of traditional home ownership: they qualify for mortgages just as easily as buyers of single-family houses, are entitled to the same tax deductions, and can sell their units at will. By contrast, the buyer of a cooperative owns shares in the building corporation, whose board of directors can restrict his right to sell.

Condos are somewhat less expensive than existing single-family houses—typically $61,698 vs. $72,962 in 1984—but they are not likely to appreciate as much. One reason is overbuilding. Housing analysts estimate that in Houston, for example, an amazing 50 percent of condos remain unsold or vacant. Moreover, as mortgage rates have eased, buyers have returned to their first love, the single-family house. According to a U.S. League of Savings Institutions report, only 8.9 percent of first-time buyers bought condos in 1983, compared with 25.6 percent in 1981.

The best condominium projects boast such appealing features as bay windows, balconies, and vaulted ceilings, all to conceal the fact that you're getting less space for your money. The median-size condominium is 1,154 square feet vs. 1,565 square feet for a typical new single-family house. The living is easy, however, because upkeep is minimal. You leave the grass cutting, snow shoveling, repairs, and other nuisances to the maintenance crew.

But you don't avoid the expense of upkeep. Residents pay a monthly maintenance fee that is likely to be consistently higher than the monthly expenses of running a house. This fee includes the cost of caring for the grounds and recreational facilities—whether you use them or not—and the price of any improvements approved by the condo board. Indeed, if you buy a condo, expect to give up some freedom. Many communities impose rules, for example, on what you can—or can't—do to the exterior of your unit, and if the bylaws say "no pets allowed," you'll probably have to leave Fido with your folks.

EXISTING HOUSES

If a house is, as the French architect Le Corbusier once said, a machine for living, then nowhere is the machinery as fine-tuned as in a home with a past. A house that's at least 10 years old has probably settled on its foundations about as much as it's going to. "You can check for major cracks in the plaster and concrete and be fairly certain that if you find none, none are likely to develop. The neighborhood has settled too. You can look at the other houses on the block and see how well the owners are caring for them. You can observe an older house in action," says real estate industry analyst Sanford Goodkin of La Jolla, California. "You're not dependent on a promise or a brochure."

Older houses have the appeal of being the kind of graceful environment where most people grew up—or wish they had. In many homes built before World War II, the quality of materials and construction surpasses that of new dwellings. You'll often find, thicker walls, full basements, and solid doors, along with lavish woodwork, high ceilings, and large rooms.

Existing houses—ones that have been sold at least once before—also tend to be less expensive than new homes. As of 1984, the average price of a 1,600-square-foot used home in a desirable neighborhood was $86,633, compared with $100,576 for a new dwelling of the same size in a similar neighborhood. For all these reasons, more than half of the people who bought their first houses in 1983 chose one that was at least 20 years old.

There are other financial advantages to older houses. As a buyer, you might be able to assume the seller's low-interest mortgage, and you will be able to estimate the cost of running the house by asking the present owner to show you bills for heating, electricity, and water. Property taxes in established neighborhoods, where streets, public utilities, schools, and sewers already exist, may be lower than in new developments where everything must be built from scratch.

You can't automatically assume that older is better, however. The wiring in such houses is often inadequate for the heavy load of contemporary appliances. The water pipes and drains may be clogged. The heating system is usually inefficient, and repairing it is expensive as well as essential for comfortable living.

NEW HOUSES

The reason that new houses appreciate faster than old ones— 43.4 percent vs. 31 percent since 1979—is simple: They're new. Usually built in areas where the population is growing, new homes are energy-efficient because local building codes now require the installation of energy-saving heating and electrical equipment as well as insulation and weather-stripping. Owners also get the latest fixtures and appliances. Should you buy the house when it is under construction, you may also be able to select the color and design of any tile, carpet, wallpaper, and paint.

New houses are getting bigger again. The median size of a newly constructed single-family dwelling was 1,565 square feet in 1983, up from 1,520 square feet in 1982. Explains Victor Mirontschuk, the Houston-based architect: "The problem with some of these small homes is that no sooner do people move in than they outgrow them."

Those builders who continue to streamline their houses are compensating for size by creating the illusion of spaciousness. Walls have come tumbling down to create so-called great rooms, which combine the space of a formal living room, dining room, family room, and even part of the kitchen into one multi-purpose open area. "What we've taken away in square footage, we've given back in design," says Santa Barbara architect Barry Berkus.

The biggest drawback to buying a new house is that you're not sure how well everything will work. You don't know whether the house will settle or how expensive it will be to maintain. One way to protect yourself is to look for such signs of high-quality construction as double-glazed windows with a sealed air space between the two panes to allow less heat to escape and less noise to enter your house. The carpentry must be neatly finished: uneven wall surfaces and moldings that don't fit are signs of shoddy workmanship. A builder warranty against structural flaws is another sign that the house is well-constructed. Currently about 30 percent of new houses have them (see "Warranties for New Houses," page 57).

FACTORY-BUILT HOUSES

Was it built in a factory or on a foundation? These days only your contractor knows for sure, since there are no telltale signs of factory construction. Once assembled, these houses look just like conventional stick-built dwellings (those built from the ground up on the site) and factory-built houses appreciate just as fast—or slowly. Last year, one-third of all new housing units were partially or totally fabricated in factories and then delivered to the sites where the pieces were put together. The advantages: lower cost and speedier construction.

Industrialized homes, as factory-built dwellings are also called, are usually sold through builder-dealers who have lots and are willing to construct the foundations and assemble the houses. But you can hire your own contractor or put the dwelling together yourself. There are four categories of industrialized housing:

Precut houses are built with logs or two-by-fours and other basic components cut and marked in a factory and then shipped to the site along with instructions on assembly. It takes three months to a year to construct a precut house, compared with six months to a year for a stick-built one, and a typical 1,725-square-foot dwelling costs $41,575 vs. $74,175 for a conventionally built house of the same size.

The pieces of a **panelized or prefabricated house** are cut and assembled into wall, roof, or floor panels at the factory before they are shipped to the site and fastened together. Panels can be ordered with only studs, wallboard, and insulation or come complete with wallpaper hung and windows installed. Depending on how finished the panels are, on-site construction takes two weeks to two months, and an average 1,725-square-foot house costs $65,000.

Modular houses arrive on the site as boxes that consist of individual rooms or groups of rooms. They are clamped together or piled up to make the house. Like their panelized relatives, the boxes can be finished at the factory with appliances, light fixtures, plumbing, wallpaper, and carpeting in place. Once on the site, a modular house can be constructed in a week, but buyers have little opportunity to modify the design. The more work that is done at the factory, the more standardization there has to be.

These homes are the most expensive type of industrialized housing, running as high as $70,725 for 1,725-square-foot units, but they are also the best made. Because they are built in plants where it is possible to control quality fairly tightly and because they travel long distances over bumpy roads to reach the site, modular homes have a reputation for being strongly constructed. "Workmen don't cut corners building modular homes at the factory," says builder Tim German of **AMCOL Development Group** in Annandale, Virginia. "They never have to rush the job because the weather is bad."

Fewer than 3 percent of **mobile homes** are going any-where these days—at least not after they are delivered from the factory to the site. Cathedral ceilings, pitched roofs, cedar siding, and bay windows have enhanced the look of permanency in these dwellings, which now conform to a national building code set by the Department of Housing and Urban Development. As a result, buyers can qualify for con-ventional 30-year mortgages instead of having to finance their purchases with installment loans. The average price of a mobile home is only $21,000, but these dwellings are not likely to appreciate as fast as other factory-built houses because their reputation has been harmed by decades of shabby construction and careless trailer-park development.

BUILDING YOUR OWN HOUSE

For most people, building your own home conjures up Frank Lloyd Wright—or one of his disciples—designing and build-ing another Falling Water. Alas, a unique, architect-designed home is out of reach for the buyer who does not have a sub-stantial income. The National Association of Home Builders estimates that a custom-built house costs up to 30 percent more than a comparable development house, even if you *don't* use an architect. If you do, his or her fee will add another 10 percent to 15 percent to the cost.

In fact, building your own home today often means just that: doing it yourself. Precut kit houses and special training schools for amateur carpenters have made it possible. According to Census Bureau figures, 179,000 homes, 17 per-cent of those built in 1983, were constructed by their owners. If you act as your own general contractor, hiring and supervising the workers yourself, you can save 20 percent of the cost of a new house. If you do most of your own work, but subcontract for the foundation and basic shell construction, you can cut the price 40 percent. And if you do everything yourself, you can save 58 percent.

There are about 40 schools around the country that will teach you the basic techniques of the building trade. The Owner Builder Center in Berkeley, California, offers four-week courses in designing, plan drawing, and home repair ($155 a couple), as well as, two-day workshops in concrete, plastering, or plumbing ($110 a person). Other teaching centers include the Yestermorrow Design/Build School in Warren, Vermont, and the Heartwood School in Washington, Massachusetts.

Few weekend workaholics realize how much effort is required to build a house from scratch. There are some 15,000 parts in any stick-built home, according to Don Carlson, the editor of the magazine *Automation in Housing and Manufactured Home Dealer.* Says he: "Anyone who pushes a pencil Monday through Friday and pounds a hammer all day Saturday may not be able to get out of bed on Sunday." Moreover, you're not likely to appreciate what the contractor does until you stand in his cement-stained shoes, juggling fire, plumbing, electrical and heating inspectors, city building ordinances, and zoning regulations.

Do-it-yourselfers may also run into trouble with financing. Before you can get a mortgage on a house, it has to be built, and before you can build it, you'll need a short-term construction loan, usually good for about nine months. But when your banker asks what you've built before and you tell him a bookcase and a birdhouse, he may not want to subsidize your nest. Kits are attractive because they solve both problems: the houses are easier for the amateur to construct, and they go up speedily enough to be built with construction loans. Says Blair Abee, director of Berkeley's Owner Builder Center: "Bankers know you're a lot less likely to blow it using a kit."

Reporter associate: Ava Plakins

Buying

Selecting the Home You Can Sell at a Profit

Robert Runde

> It's hard to beat the resale value of a traditional house in a stable neighborhood.

In the '80s, a house is just a home—not the inflation-buster it might have been in the '70s. High interest rates coupled with moderate inflation have slowed the wallet-popping appreciation in real estate. Since 1981, for example, the median resale price of a single-family house has risen less than 10 percent, and in cities such as Fort Lauderdale and San Jose, California, property values are dropping.

Nonetheless, your house is still the largest investment you are likely to make, so you need to buy carefully. Since the circumstances under which you'd make a killing are exceptional, a more realistic goal is to look for a place that will hold its value by keeping up with inflation. Before you buy a house today, says Jack Frost, an executive vice president of the national real estate firm Coldwell Banker, "You need to balance its livability with its resale value, in about 75 percent to 25 percent proportions." As it happens, the qualities that make for livability are very often the same ones that enable a house to maintain its value in the resale market.

As a buyer looking for a house that will appreciate, your first consideration should be price. Because inflation is unlikely to bail you out, it no longer makes sense to mortgage yourself to the eyeballs and buy more house than you can afford. And if that borrowing comes in the form of an adjustable-rate mortgage, your monthly payments will go up year after year if interest rates rise. Says Fran Wiehn, who owns ERA Realty Specialists in Groton, Connecticut: "You don't want to buy a house and then have to eat hot dogs and beans for the rest of your life." Moreover, you'll be at a disadvantage when you are ready to sell the house if you cannot afford to keep the place up. Anne Arnold, a real estate agent with the William F. Higgins Agency in Hillsdale, New Jersey, notes: "If you don't have the money to paint your house or put on a new roof, you'll never get top dollar for it."

The best way to stretch your money is to buy the neighborhood rather than the house. The next chapter will help you pick a desirable community. Once you've settled on an area, look for the ugly duckling on a street full of swans. "Even if the buyer doesn't improve his property," says Jim Droz, a Newhall, California, real estate agent, the neighborhood will pull its value up."

What you don't want is the most expensive house on the block. Three years ago, a California physician moved to Paducah, Kentucky, and paid $145,000 for a French provincial house surrounded by smaller houses worth only $65,000 to $80,000. A year later, having sunk an additional $8,000 into renovations, the doctor moved back to California and put the house on the market for $149,000. It finally sold—after nine months—for $120,000.

Restoring an older house with architectural interest can dramatically increase its worth. In many parts of the country, antiquarian touches such as stained-glass windows, natural wood floors, and gingerbread trim enhance property values. Notes Joseph Benoit, who owns his own real estate firm in Somerville, Massachusetts: "Younger people, especially, seem to enjoy houses with charm and character. Around here, the market pays for plaster medallions in the center of a ceiling."

You can also try to better your lot by going to the other extreme and putting your money into a brand-new tract house. "Until they get the first few houses off their hands and realize that everything's going to be all right, builders are very anxious," says Fran Wiehn, the Groton, Connecticut, real estate agent. Savvy buyers can capitalize on those fears not only to knock down the asking price but also to squeeze extras out of the contractor—an attic fan, for example, or better-quality kitchen fixtures.

Such rewards will help compensate you for the discombobulations of living amid the din of construction and taking your own garbage to the dump at least until the streets are paved. In 1983 Harry and Debbie Smith bought a four-bedroom colonial in Sterling, Virginia, when few houses in the subdivision had been built. The price: $96,950. By the time the Smiths moved in a year later, the same model as theirs was going for $104,000.

If you are one of the first buyers in a development, you may pay less for it than later owners will pay. But you are taking a risk. "If other houses don't sell, your investment could turn out to be not so good," says Sandra Wayson of Equitable Relocation Management Corp. in Orlando, Florida. Therefore she suggests that before you commit yourself, you visit the builder's earlier developments, knock on a few doors and ask owners about how well his houses have sold.

Buy a conventional house in a well-established locality if you are neither a remodeler nor a risk taker. Avoid the unusual. Says Michael Cannon, president of Appraisal & Real Estate Economics Associates in Miami: "Most buyers want a traditional style in a stable, mature neighborhood." Although the favored style varies from place to place, the houses that hold their value best fall into one of three categories: colonials, ranches, and split-levels. In the center of the country, a one-and-a-half story variation of the colonial known as the midwestern traditional is popular. Contemporaries—one-story boxlike ranch houses with no trim or shutters and a long roof overhang—are more common in the South and West.

Whether you buy a colonial or a contemporary, an old house or a new one, the interior has to be fairly standard. Now that families are smaller, a three-bedroom house is easier to resell than one with four or more. Your domicile should have at least two full baths and preferably a powder room as well. The smallest room in the house receives serious scrutiny these days, and such luxurious fixtures as double sinks, oversize tubs, and skylights appeal to buyers.

The way a house is laid out—that is, the size and position of the rooms in relation to one another—can affect its resale price. Says W. Bruce Wallin, vice president of Homerica, a national house-finding service based in Danbury, Connecticut: "A place that still has a tiny nook of a kitchen, even though a family room and extra bedroom have been added, won't sell easily." New rooms should not look like afterthoughts or disrupt the flow of traffic in the house. A powder room off the kitchen won't be accessible to guests, for instance, unless that kitchen has been enlarged to include a family room.

If the floor plan is well thought out, however, it does not have to be rigidly traditional. The newest trend, which is catching on especially fast in the sunbelt, is the so-called split-plan house. The master-bedroom suite is on one side, common living areas are in the middle, and the children's quarters are on the far side. Both generations retain some privacy that way.

You can't disguise a dog of a house with one or two spectacular features, but a modern kitchen can make up for a lot that is missing elsewhere. Buyers feel strongly about the galley. It doesn't have to be equipped for *haute cuisine* but it should certainly be appealing and come with a number of appliances. Dishwashers and garbage disposals are virtual necessities, and microwave ovens, though still uncommon, are rapidly gaining in popularity. Amenities go in and out of style, unfortunately, and nowadays buyers are unwilling to pay for walk-in pantries or cooktop islands.

Some fixtures are always in fashion. Fireplaces, though wasteful of energy, are romantic accessories treasured even in warm parts of the country. Alas, home is no longer where the hearth is for many cost-conscious developers. Slightly more than half the new houses built last year had fireplaces, compared with almost two-thirds in 1978.

The surest way to maximize your resale value is to shop for quality in the first place. Last year Ron and Susan Quinn sold their $91,000 tract house in the San Diego suburb of Spring Valley and bought an older home in the city for $125,000. They were attracted to its hardwood floors, cove moldings, tile fireplace, and brass fixtures. Says Susan: "This was built as a simple house 40 years ago, but expensive new homes today are flimsy by comparison. This place is so much more solid than a new one that I know it will increase its value."

Reporter associate: Martha Mader

Checklist

Most people buy houses with their hearts, not their heads, so you have to train yourself to become passionate about the right kind of home. Ask yourself the following 10 questions; five no answers mean you love unwisely:

☐ Can I keep up the payments on my adjustable-rate mortgage if interest rates rise next year?

☐ Will I have enough money left over to maintain the house?

☐ Is the house in keeping with the neighborhood?

☐ If the house is unique, does it have historic interest?

☐ Am I willing to repair a dilapidated house?

☐ Will fixing it up improve the resale value?

☐ Do I find the rooms where I expect them to be?

☐ Are the rooms easily accessible from all parts of the house?

☐ Does the house have a fireplace?

☐ Are the kitchen appliances modern and in working order?

The First Step: Picking the Right Location

Robert Runde

> The neighborhood you choose
> can be even more important
> than the house.

If you carted your house from place to place on a flatbed
truck, you'd be startled at how its value would vary. Take
two Boston suburbs, for example. Local real estate agents
estimate that a three-bedroom, two-bath Victorian house in
good condition would cost around $120,000 in working-class
Somerville. Four miles to the west, in upper-middle-class
Belmont, the same house would command about $220,000.
As any real estate agent will tell you, location matters more
than the house itself.

Not only do neighboring communities in a metropolitan
area often differ greatly in their desirability, but also some
cities enjoy more rapid real estate appreciation than others.
The leaders are usually places where booming local econo-
mies create disposable income, which in turn pushes up
house prices. Property values will rise fastest in the coming
years in Colorado Springs, Dallas-Fort Worth, and Har-
risburg, Pennsylvania, predicts Alfred Gobar of Brea, California, a nationally known real estate consultant.
Conversely, he believes, houses in Cleveland, Honolulu, and
Houston will appreciate slowly.

Unfortunately, if your job is in Houston, you can't very

well live in Dallas. And trying to zero in on the community in your area that will be the best investment can be difficult. Fortunately, you can get professional help in sorting out the possibilities. Corporations hire such national companies as Merrill Lynch Relocation Management or Homerica of Danbury, Connecticut, to assist their transferred executives. The Employee Relocation Council (1627 K St. N.W., Washington, D.C. 20006) can supply the names of other organizations that work with companies to aid transferees.

The council can also direct you to one of several relocation specialists that work with poeple who are moving on their own. For example, more than 1,300 real estate brokers are affiliated with RELO, the Intercity Relocation Service Inc. (Suite 1200, 230 N. Michigan Ave., Chicago, Ill. 60601), an association of independent realty firms that serve people moving to a new town. You don't pay a fee when you employ a RELO agent, who counts on receiving a commission for selling you a house.

If you are well-organized and diligent, you can mount the search for the right community yourself. That's what Robert Bajema and his wife Marlena do. Now Seattle branch manager for IBM's national marketing division, Bajema, 37, and his wife have been transferred five times during the past nine years. IBM provides relocation assistance, but the Bajemas feel they can do a more thorough job on their own.

Before the Bajemas settle in a new area, they visit municipal government offices and ask city planners which suburbs and parts of cities are growing fastest. Though their children, aged nine and 11, are still young, the Bajemas interview principals, teachers, and parents looking for school systems that stress college preparatory education. They also consult with builders, real estate agents, and business acquaintances.

The Bajemas want a neighborhood where the houses are all roughly the same age and condition. And they like to be near high-quality entertainment and shopping as well as within an easy commute of Bob's office. In 1983 they spent about two months evaluating neighborhoods before they bought a $216,000 four-bedroom contemporary in Issaquah, 14 miles east of Seattle. Says Bajema: "Research is essential. If you do your homework before you buy, you'll make out just fine when you sell."

The first winnowing you do should be for price. Leafing

through multiple-listing service books in real estate brokers' offices and inspecting a few houses will quickly give you an idea which communities are out of reach. Once you have decided on the areas you can afford, the local school systems should be your next concern, whether or not you have children. When it is time to sell your house, you'll discover that superior schools are the top priority among buyers. When Jim Peck was transferred by Memorex Corp. from Dallas to San Jose, California, last summer, he and his wife Vicky spent $349,000 for a suburban Saratoga house with four minute bedrooms and a kitchen in need of modernization. That was more money for less house then they wanted. The Pecks, whose son Kevin is an eighth-grader, paid up because the school system is the best in the area, Peck contends. "And that's why Saratoga has had steady appreciation in home prices, even while properties in other places around San Jose have been declining."

When you become interested in a particular community, spend as much time as you can investigating its school system. You can't measure schools scientifically, but some statistics are useful. For example, 94 percent of Saratoga High School's seniors went on to college last year vs. a national average of 54 percent. Scholastic Aptitude Test scores are also indicative of the quality of a school system. The students in affluent Scarsdale, New York, averaged 532 on the verbal portion of the SAT last year and 583 on the math section. In Mamaroneck, a similarly prosperous community nearby, the comparable scores were 490 and 520, closer to the national averages of 426 and 471.

Another favorable sign is local support for the public schools. In places where voters must approve school budgets, ask how referendums have fared in recent years. A call to the superintendent of schools or board of education will produce that information. At the same time, check on the districting of students. Will your kids go to schools close by or will they have to ride buses? If one school has a better reputation than another, consider concentrating your house search within its district. This is most important if you have junior high or high school age children who will be applying to colleges in a few years. In evaluating secondary schools, look for programs to meet individual needs. If you are fairly certain that your kids will be going to college, search for a school system that will best prepare them for it. For example, each year at Edina

High School in suburban Minneapolis, where college-level courses are emphasized, 35 percent of 11th- and 12th-graders take accelerated classes and qualify for college credits.

● ther municipal services should be topflight also, and it's easy to satisfy yourself that they are. Is garbage picked up at the back door or do residents have to lug it to the street? Are the roads smooth or rutted with axle-threatening potholes? Do residents boast about the local library, the speedy snow removal, and the efficient fire department? Do the police have any special programs to combat crime? In many places, they conduct voluntary fingerprinting programs for young children to discourage kidnapping.

Economic vitality is another key ingredient in an attractive town. Ask the local Chamber of Commerce for names of communities with low unemployment and a number of corporate headquarters. This information is particularly important for two-income couples where one spouse has been transferred and the other has to find a new job.

There is a quick way to find out how attractive other people think a community is: Look at the variation between the asking and the selling prices of the houses. In choice areas, the difference is small; often the house sells for just 3 percent to 5 percent less than the owners asked. Another yardstick is how long houses are on the market; fewer than three months means the area is in demand. To get these data, call either the local Board of Realtors or the home builders' association.

You can't be completely cold-blooded in your calculation of value though; your personal likes and dislikes are also important. Pat Mead, a consultant who helps people move into the Cleveland area, suggests that you "make sure you and your family will be comfortable with an area's conveniences or—if it is a remote suburb—with its isolation." If you work in Reno, for instance, will you mind the 45-minute drive required to enjoy the ambience of living at Lake Tahoe? Can you tolerate the urban congestion of Stamford, Connecticut, in return for its proximity to jobs, excellent shopping, and unusually fine cultural and recreational facilities?

Once you have picked a town, finding the right neighborhood is an easier task. Begin by talking with real estate agents and driving around; you're likely to get very definite feelings about different places. Even so, neighborhoods that appeal to you will probably share many characteristics. All the houses will be approximately equal in value, for instance. Avoid areas where there's a wide disparity because a number of smaller, cheaper dwellings can pull down the prices of their more elaborate neighbors. Careless zoning also erodes property values; you don't want to find auto body shops or mobile homes mingling with single-family houses. A keen eye as you drive through a community will probably tell you as much as you need to know about how conscientiously it has been zoned. However, if you are concentrating on a particular house or neighborhood and want to know whether that charming farm next door has been rezoned for light industry, a visit to the municipality's planning office would be in order.

As you drive around a neighborhood, look for neatly trimmed lawns and hedges, well-tended gardens, and healthy trees. A community that is fastidiously maintained adds value to a house. Says W. Bruce Wallin, vice president of Homerica, the national house-finding service: "If all the houses and yards are well cared for, you can bet the neighbors are thinking about resale."

You'll take the least risk buying a conventional-looking house in a well-kept middle- or upper-class neighborhood filled with homes just like yours. When Dr. Veronica K. Yates moved from Tulsa to Cleveland last fall to become assistant director of occupational health at Standard Oil of Ohio, she was determined to buy a large house with a view of Lake Erie. She found a 44-year-old five-bedroom colonial with an unobstructed view of the water in the Lakewood section. The house cost her $230,000, which local real estate agents say is a bargain in a neighborhood boasting turn-of-the-century homes on streets lined with sycamores and maples. Says she: "I'm counting on my house to hold its value so I'll have money later for a smaller house and for my retirement."

If you are willing to gamble, you may be able to find a house that will appreciate at a better-than-average pace in a section of a city that is out of favor but has the potential for a comeback. The risk is that what you thought was an up-and-coming neighborhood is actually down-and-going. That's why you might limit your pioneering to areas where some houses have already been renovated.

Being a successful urban homesteader usually takes gritty determination and time. Three years ago, Stan and Carol Harris bought a run-down, 90-year-old Queen Anne-style house in the once fancy, now neglected West Adams section of Los Angeles. Other houses were being rehabilitated nearby, but theirs needed extensive work. The house cost just $67,000, however, in a city where the median price of existing houses was $115,484.

In September, 1984, $40,000 later, the Harrises finished their renovations. They weren't expecting to see an immediate payoff on their investment, but in February, 1985, they received an offer of $150,000, a 40 percent return on their total investment.

So as you trudge from place to place, let your instincts help guide your investment decision. Ask yourself: "Would I be proud to live here?" Chances are, if you would be, so would future buyers.

Checklist
With houses, where *you buy is usually more important than* what *you buy. To find the right neighborhood, you should judge promising communities according to these qualities:*

☐ Schools. How old are the facilities? Does the community have a history of giving schools financial support? Do a very high percentage—80 percent or so—of high school seniors go to college? Do their scores on national tests compare favorably with those of students in neighboring school districts?

☐ Municipal services. Does the community seem clean? Does it offer such services as back-door garbage pickup or special police programs to keep crime in check? Is the neighborhood on the sewer line?

☐ Transportation. Are highways efficient and in repair? Is there reliable mass transit?

☐ Amenities. Is there good shopping nearby? Are recreational and cultural facilities close at hand?

☐ Ambience. Do houses and yards seem well-maintained? Has the business district been kept up? Do you see evidence of careful zoning, or do homes and commercial establishments mingle haphazardly?

Once Over Thoroughly

William C. Banks

> Before you buy, inspect a house
> carefully to avoid costly
> problems later.

Whether the dwelling of your dreams is Victorian or so new the windows still have the manufacturer's stickers on them, inspecting it thoroughly before you buy may save you thousands of dollars and a paralyzing case of buyer's remorse. To detect the hidden flaws, you'll need a handful of inexpensive tools: a flashlight, a screwdriver, a pair of binoculars, a marble, and an electrical outlet analyzer. The outlet analyzer, a plug-in device about the size of a saltshaker, sells for around $10 at most hardware stores. If you don't own binoculars, borrow a pair from a friend; if necessary, steal the marble from a small child. The tools will provide the answers to questions raised by your other self, the deeply suspicious one who is afraid the house you adore is a fraud.

Before you start snooping around, you should know what to look for and how much repairs are likely to cost. Or you can hire a professional home inspector at $150 to $300 and accompany him as he does your looking for you. An experienced investigator will certainly see more than even the most careful amateur. Says M.B. Williams, former executive director of the American Society of Home Inspectors, "An inspector is not your appraiser, he's your informer. He gives you the facts so you can make an intelligent decision about a fair price for the house and the costs of fixing it up."

You can write to the society (Suite 320, 655 15th St. N.W.,

Washington, D.C. 20005) for the names of members in your area. Select a company that has been in business locally for at least three years, and ask for references from satisfied customers.

Don't hesitate to call in a home inspector if you doubt your ability to recognize and evaluate major signs of trouble. A professional opinion is also in order if your own inspection reveals serious flaws or if you're puzzled by what you've found. An inspector scrutinizes more than 75 items, from the chimney cap to the sewer drainpipe, and he'll usually estimate the costs of repairs.

No matter who will be conducting the investigation, make sure your sales contract is contingent upon the house passing a thorough inspection. The house won't get a perfect score from an inspector, but if you find that you must make costly repairs, you may want to negotiate a lower sale price or get out of the contract.

Arrange with the seller for about three hours of purposeful prowling, and begin with a stroll around the grounds. Two of the most serious outdoor problems are improper grading around the foundation of the house and depressions in the lawn within 25 feet of the dwelling. Both result in rainwater collecting around the foundation, where dampness can cause flooding in the basement.

The ground next to the foundation should slope away from the house for at least six feet, deflecting water from it. Typically, you'll pay $300 to $800 to regrade an average suburban house—that is, to build up the slope of the soil to direct water away from the foundation. Poor drainage may cause water to flow underground, where it can exert potentially damaging pressure on the foundation walls. Plan to pay a landscape company about $17 an hour per person to dig ditches in a swamplike yard and install drainage pipes.

Evaluating the house itself is largely a matter of determining how well it will protect you from nature and how reliable the plumbing, electrical, and heating systems are. As a rule, new houses aren't afflicted with the structural ills that beset many older homes, but some new houses suffer from shoddy workmanship and inferior materials.

As you walk around inside a new house, look for low-quality items such as hollow-core wood doors, thin metal sliding doors on closets, and single-thickness window glass instead of double-glazed thermal panes. If you have to add storm windows, plan on spending between $50 and $80 a window.

Take note of the appliances: to cut costs, builders frequently install bottom-of-the-line models. If you don't recognize the brand name on the stove, dishwasher, or washing machine, or if a dearth of buttons and chrome suggests a spartan issue, negotiate for higher-quality gear. A builder who has other new homes under construction can usually install new appliances in a matter of hours. Even if you decide to keep the no-frills machines, raise them as an issue to bargain down the price of the house.

Be on the lookout for damage caused by careless workers. Chips in Formica counters, sinks, tubs, and woodwork should be repaired before you move in. The carpeting should fit snugly and have no discernible seams. If joint tape is visible anywhere on walls and ceilings, or if the paint doesn't cover the walls properly, demand that the builder redo the finish work. The entire house should be spotless: sparkling windows, no paint or plaster drops on cabinets and floors, and no dust.

What you don't see in the house can be just as important as visible flaws. For example, in their haste to move on to the next job, workers have been known to forget to install the baseboards, the insulation in the attic, and the caulking around the bathtub. And make certain that the builder hasn't neglected to put in that air-conditioning system you were promised; an oversight like that could cost you $3,000 later.

Be sure to write down all the flaws. Says home inspector Kent Boucher, vice president of Claxton Walker & Associates in Potomac, Maryland: "If you present the builder with a list of problems before you settle in, you usually get the work done quickly. After that, it's a matter of discussion, and that can take time, especially if the builder's moved on to another job."

A house that is more than 15 years old requires closer scrutiny than a new one. After all, some old homes have been standing out in the rain and cold since the days when George Washington was remodeling Mount Vernon. The enemies of an old house are subtle, devious foes: deterioration and water.

The outdoor inspection of an older house must include a close look at nearby trees. Limbs hanging over the roof will have to be trimmed because they might break off and damage it during a storm. Diseased or dead trees will also have to be cut down, and the average cost of removing a tree is about $1,000.

Examine masonry walls, walks, driveways, and patios for cracks and mortar deterioration. Poke joints with the screwdriver; if mortar crumbles easily, it's time for repairs. Masons charge $12 to $18 an hour. Expect to pay about $700 to replace a 25-foot concrete walk. Look for tilting or bulging in the retaining walls, the masonry bulwarks that hold back the earth and form terraces in the yard. If the distortions are obvious at a glance, call in a structural engineer and brace yourself for a repair estimate of several thousand dollars. While you're outside, use your binoculars to look for rust, holes, or leaks in the gutters and downspouts. They're a vital line of defense against water damage. Professionals charge about $3 a linear foot to install new gutters; that's roughly $500 for a three-bedroom ranch-style house.

When you scan the roof through the binoculars, check for cracked or worn shingles. For example, curled or buckled asphalt shingles with dark, barren spots should be replaced immediately. If such deterioration is visible on more than half the shingles, the house may need a new roof within a year. Cost: about $ 2,500 for a 2,000-square-foot roof. Finally, examine the flashing—the metal strips between roof slopes and around the tops of dormers and the base of the chimney. Twisted or broken flashing often results in leaks, and most roofers charge about $30 an hour to replace and reseal it.

Use the screwdriver—gingerly—to check for damage in outside walls. Gentle probing into discolored patches on wood siding and mortar joints between bricks should reveal rotten or deteriorated spots. One or two rotten clapboards or deteriorated mortar around a few score bricks can usually be fixed by a carpenter or mason for less than $300. Also inspect outside walls for thin, branchlike mud tubes; these are termite freeways leading from nests in the ground to the appetizing wood beams that support the house. Probe infested areas with your screwdriver to check the extent of the damage. The average cost of extermination: $700. If you've set your heart on a house that has exterior decay over more than about 10 square feet, or all along the lowest few feet of an entire wall, call in a professional inspector or a structural engineer no matter how good the condition of the rest of the house.

Begin your indoor inspection at the top. If the attic is only a crawl space under the roof, take a look up there with your flashlight. You should see air vents or some mechanical venting devices that allow moist air to escape and at least six inches of insulation between the attic floor beams to keep heat in. Installing fiberglass insulation is a messy job that you could do yourself, but no one would blame you if you paid a professional about 50¢ a square foot to do it for you. Insulating the walls and ceiling of a finished attic may require cutting through a wall and crawling around in cramped quarters; a professional won't like it anymore than you would, so he may charge a premium.

Next, train your flashlight on the inside of the roof. Look for dark stains and rust trails from nails, both signs of leaks. A few small leaks are no cause for alarm, especially if the shingles seem fine, but a heavy, damp mark or mildew may mean a patch is needed. If it looks like a large leak has been left unattended for some time, expect to find water stains in ceilings and on walls below.

When you come downstairs, check all rooms for cracks in walls and ceilings, and open windows and doors to make sure they work properly. If you're thinking of refinishing hardwood floors, make sure the floorboards haven't already been sanded down excessively. Visible nailheads and a one-eighth-inch declivity in the flooring along the baseboards are bad signs; unsanded flooring may also be visible in corners and under radiators. If you sand again, gaps between boards will yawn and nailheads will gleam from wall to wall. Place your marble in the center of the floor in every carpetless room. If the marble rolls swiftly to a wall, you've found a tilted floor, which can be a sign of serious structural problems. When accompanied by cracks around doorjambs and window frames, doors that don't close easily, and windows that jam halfway, a fast-rolling marble augurs ill. Your aggie may not roll in a carpeted room, but cracks around door frames and misaligned doors and windows should be enough to kindle your suspicion.

In houses that are more than 25 years old, you should check for clogged water pipes by turning on a tap in the uppermost bathroom. Testing first the cold water, next the hot, open the sink taps fully and let them run. Then with your eye on the sink faucets, open the bathtub taps. If the flow into the sink suddenly drops more than about 25 percent, it's likely that corrosion inside the pipes is restricting flow and you'll probably need major repairs within five years. Cost: up to $1,400 for a house with two baths.

Count the electrical outlets in every room, and test each one with the plug-in analyzer. An electrician will charge about $50 to $75 to install a couple of new outlets. Test all appliances to make sure they're in working order.

In the basement, watermarks along the walls suggest flooding. Watch out for a freshly painted basement: the owners may be trying to disguise the evidence. A wet basement's exact cause is notoriously difficult to diagnose. The solution might be as simple and inexpensive as correcting a misaligned downspout that has been sluicing water from the gutters into the ground next to the foundation. Or the job could be as drastic as excavating the entire foundation and waterproofing the foundation walls. That will run to several thousand dollars for most homes. Don't take chances with a wet basement. Call in a professional inspector or an engineer. If the expert is worried, deduct the estimated cost of repair from the selling price or look for another house.

Bulges in the basement walls accompanied by horizontal cracks more than a quarter of an inch wide suggest that pressure around the foundation may be greater than the walls can stand. Call in an inspector before you buy the house. A few small vertical cracks, especially those filled with dust or the remains of generations of spiders, might only be evidence that the house eased itself into a more comfortable position many years ago. Look for little piles of sawdust near the beams. They are evidence of wood-boring insects, such as carpenter ants. Exterminators typically charge about $700 to rid a dwelling of these and other insects.

The basement is also the best place to judge the condition of the electrical wiring. Look for frayed or loose wires attached to overhead beams. Open the door to the square metal electrical box, which is usually on the wall in plain sight. Scorch marks around fuses and a burning smell are signs of an electrical overload; for boxes with circuit breakers, check for a burning smell around the outlets. Look on the inside of the door for a label stating the house voltage and amperage. As a rule, a house needs 240 volts. Amperage must be about 100 for a house that uses gas for cooking and heating, 200 amperes for an all-electric home. An electrician charges $600 to $750 to upgrade the power supply.

No matter what the weather, run the furnace for at least 15 minutes. When it's roaring, remove the front panel and look inside. Heavy oil stains on the floor or a wobbling gas flame are signs of an old and tired heating system. The average life span of oil-fired furnaces is 35 years, gas furnaces, 25 years. A new furnace costs between $1,200 and $2,200. While you're at it, examine the inside of the furnace frame for rust or watermarks. Wily owners who've spruced up the basement to disguise signs of flooding usually forget to clean inside the furnace frame.

The water heater—a white cylindrical tank about four feet tall—is usually located near the furnace. Check around the base for rust chips; they're an indication of deterioration. The average life of a water heater is 10 years. Replacement cost: $200 to $400 for a 40-gallon unit, big enough to ensure hot showers for a family of four.

When you complete your inspection, take your list of all the flaws you've discovered to local contractors to confirm your repair estimates. Add up the costs and use the sum to bargain down the price of the house.

Checklist

The following areas warrant special scrutiny in any home more than 10 years old. The repair prices cited are average for most parts of the country.

- [ ] The roof: replacing 100 square feet of worn-out asphalt shingles costs $125; wood shake, $400; slate, $600.
- [ ] Gutters and downspouts: replacement cost is $3 a linear foot.
- [ ] Water pipes: expect to pay $1,400 to replace clogged or leaky supply pipes in a two-bath house.
- [ ] Furnace: a new oil-fired furnace usually costs $1,700 to $2,200; gas, $1,200 to $2,000.
- [ ] Water heater: a new 40-gallon water heater costs between $200 and $400.
- [ ] Air conditioning: a gas-fired central air-conditioning system costs $2,000 to $3,000; an electric system, about $1,800.

☐ Storm windows: expect to pay about $80 a window installed.

☐ Floor refinishing: sanding, staining, and sealing a hardwood floor costs $1.50 a square foot.

☐ Insulation: expect to spend 50¢ a square foot for professionally installed attic insulation.

☐ Electricity: to update and upgrade the power supply, you'll pay $700. Rewiring a typical two-story, four-bedroom house costs $2,000 to $5,000.

What a Real Estate Agent Does for You

Kay Williams

> He'll tell you about houses and mortgages, but he works for the seller, not the buyer.

When you get serious about shopping for a new house, you'll probably pick up the Sunday paper, find an ad for a charming three-bedroom contemporary in a location that appeals to you, and call the agent in the ad. The chances are slim that you'll buy the first house you see. The relationship you establish with the agent who shows it to you, however, is likely to be a lasting one. He may have to take you through many more houses before you settle on the place to buy.

If you are lucky, the agent you find through the classifieds will be just right—well-acquainted with the local housing market, perceptive about your family's needs and familiar with various types of mortgages and how you can qualify for them. But to choose the person who is knowledgeable enough to guide you through what is likely to be the biggest expenditure of your life, you need more than luck and a newspaper.

The terms real estate broker, real estate agent, and realtor are often confused, but what each does is not always interchangeable. An agent is the person you will deal with most; he works for a broker, who has attained that status by meeting strict state licensing standards and working for several years as an agent himself. Both the agent and the broker may call themselves realtors; that term signifies that they are members of the National Association of Realtors, a trade organization. While the title realtor is no guarantee of a salesman's abilities, it does at least indicate that he subscribes to the association's code of ethics.

To find a competent agent who represents an outstanding brokerage firm, look first in your own backyard. If you have friends who have recently moved to the area you are interested in, get referrals from them; if they were pleased with their agents, chances are you will be too. Or you can telephone the local Board of Realtors and ask for the names of several former Realtors of the Year. They earn this designation on the basis of successful salesmanship and knowledge of legislative and financial matters related to their field.

Local offices of national franchises, such as Gallery of Homes and Century 21, will refer you to other offices if you are moving to a new area. The firm will usually be reputable, and if you don't like the agent assigned to you, you can request another. You can also attend open houses, held on designated days during which a broker allows the general public to view several of the homes listed for sale with his firm. Regardless of whether you like the houses, you will get to know the agents showing them, and they will have other dwellings to sell.

The agent should have access to the local multiple-listing service, a computerized network that gives him a complete rundown of all houses listed for sale in the area through the service. A good agent will spend weeks or months showing you and your family dozens of properties. It is in your best interest—as well as his—to establish a ceiling on what you can afford to avoid wasting time looking at properties that are out of your price range.

You should expect your agent to show you all the houses that you might want to buy. The National Association of Realtors discourages a practice known as steering, in which an agent shows—or doesn't show—certain properties to minority groups. If you suspect that you are being steered by an agent, or you want to make sure that you won't be, look for someone known as a realtist. Realtists belong to the National Association of Real Estate Brokers (1101 14th St. N.W., Suite 1000, Washington, D.C. 20005; 202-289-6655), an organization that promotes minorities' rights in real estate.

An agent will help you determine how much house you can carry based on your income and other expenses, using the same standards a bank employs to determine how big a mortgage you can afford. Once you've found the place you want to buy, he will recommend a professional inspector to examine the soundness of the structure. Finally, he will help "you negotiate the price and close the sale."

The brokerage firm that handles the sale earns a commission of 6 percent of the selling price of a house for listing it—that is, putting it on the market—and selling it. If your broker is from another firm, the commission is usually split 50-50 between the broker who lists the house and your broker. The real estate agent's cut is paid out of his broker's share.

A seller pays the commission from the proceeds of the sale, and the bottom line is this: the brokers and agents work for him. Real estate practice is set up to favor the seller. For that reason never tell an agent, "Let's offer the Smiths $100,000 on their house, then we'll go as high as $110,000 if we have to." He is obliged by industry custom to repeat that information to the seller or his agent. Wait until the seller refuses your first offer before you volunteer that you are willing to spend more.

The conflict of interest faced by an agent can be even more acute when he is also the listing agent responsible for the sale of the property. Then he represents both buyer and seller during negotiations. Quite frankly, he can pressure you into paying more for the house than it is worth in order to earn his commission. As a practical matter, an agent doesn't usually make this mistake. He might not drive as hard a bargain with the seller as you would, but he's not likely to cheat you either. The reason is simple: someday you are going to sell that house and buy another one. Explains Montgomery, Alabama, broker John Walter Stowers, Jr.: "We want the repeat business."

The potential for double-dealing is exacerbated when the housing market is tight, as it is, for example, in Los Angeles and New York City. But you can protect yourself by hiring a buyer's broker. A buyer's broker is licensed to sell real estate but represents only the buyer. He can accept listings, but he should not show you those houses. Explains Sloan L. Bashinsky, a buyer's broker and author of *Home Buyers: Lambs to the Slaughter* (Simon & Schuster, $12.95): "That would result in an even worse conflict of interest. He'd be paid twice." A buyer's broker can charge you a percentage of the purchase price or a flat fee that is usually equal to about half the standard commission. But most bill by the hour—usually $60 to $75—and that is the best arrangement for you because the broker will then have no incentive to guide you toward more expensive properties to increase his fee.

Buyer's brokers can open up the entire local housing market for you. Not only do they have access to the multiple-listing system, but they also can assist with the purchase of homes offered for sale by their owners. A traditional agent will have little luck interesting an independent seller in showing you his home. If you buy the house, the seller is obligated to pay the agent a commission. But a buyer's broker has the same entrée to these houses that you do, since you, not the seller, are paying his fee.

As your representative he will be sure to recommend that a home under serious consideration for purchase gets a thorough going-over by a professional inspector. He can get a copy of the deed, and the information in it—what the seller paid for the house, how long he's owned it, and any outstanding liens—will give you an edge in bargaining over the price. That way, during the negotiations, you shouldn't have to worry about conflict of interest because one broker clearly works for the buyer and one for the seller.

There's another service the buyer's broker renders when necessary—reining in the purchaser. "When you fall in love with a house, you tend to lose sight of what it's actually worth and what you can afford," says Sloan Bashinsky. "You need somebody to slow you down, bring you back to earth and protect you from yourself."

There are currently only 6,000 buyer's brokers across the country, compared with at least a million traditional brokers and agents, but their numbers are growing. To find one, ask your local Board of Realtors, a title insurance company, or a real estate attorney for names. Or send $25 to *Who's Who in Creative Real Estate* (921 E. Main St., Suite F, Ventura, Calif. 93001) for a national directory of some 1,200 buyer's brokers. And given a choice between an independent buyer's broker or one affiliated with a large real estate agency, go with the little guy.

Buying

Checklist

Before you search for a house, look for a broker. Don't depend on luck and newspaper ads to find him; do the following as well:

☐ Ask friends for recommendations.

☐ Get referrals from the local Board of Realtors and branches of national franchises and attend open houses.

☐ Question the agent about the housing market in the neighborhood that interests you.

☐ Ask if the agent has access to a multiple-listing service so that you can be sure of seeing as many houses as possible.

☐ Establish a price range with the agent so he will not show you houses you can't afford.

☐ Wait for the seller's counteroffer before you tell the agent that you'd be willing to pay more for the house.

☐ Consider hiring a buyer's broker to assist you in your search. He will represent you, thus ensuring you against conflicts between the buying agent and the selling agent.

Getting the Best Mortgage

Robert Runde

> Money is plentiful, but you have to choose between fixed and adjustable rates.

Choosing a mortgage is no longer a matter of simply finding the lowest interest rate. Now you have to sort through a baffling variety of products with varying rates, terms, and fees. Globe Mortgage Co. of Hackensack, New Jersey, for example, proudly boasts 28 different types of mortgages—"just like Howard Johnson's ice cream," says senior vice president James Richmond.

As you browse among mortgages, your attention will naturally be drawn to interest rates. They began dropping steadily and early in 1985, rates on conventional fixed-rate loans typically ranged from 12½ percent to 13 percent, while adjustable-rate mortgages, known as ARMs, were offered at rates below 10 percent. With an adjustable, your interest rate and monthly payments fluctuate with the movements in whatever index the loan is linked to.

All else being equal, you'd grab that lower rate, of course. But *nothing* is equal in the mortgage market anymore. Depending on whether your bank, savings and loan, or other lender wants to make fixed- or adjustable-rate loans, you'll pay higher fees for the type the lender is least enthusiastic about. Fees are figured in points, with each point equal to 1 percent of your loan amount; for example, one point on a $75,000 mortgage is $750.

The way to compare different types of loans is to have the

lender figure out for you the annual percentage rate (APR), which includes points, that you'll pay in each case. Lenders are required by federal law to disclose the APR—the effective interest rate a borrower pays. For example, the APR could tell you which of two $80,000 mortgages recently offered by a New York City savings bank is more attractive— a fixed rate at 12⅞ percent with $1,600 in fees or a one-year adjustable at an introductory rate of 9¾ percent, 14 percent in the second year, and $2,000 in charges. Answer: the fixed rate. Its effective rate is 13.26 percent vs. 13.63 percent for the adjustable.

Once you have put different mortgages on the same interest-rate footing, you'll be able to judge the best one more accurately. However, the lender will often make the choice for you, based on your income, your current debt load, and the size loan you need. You may find that you cannot qualify for any kind of mortgage if you would wind up spending more than 28 percent of your gross income on housing costs, including principal repayment, interest, taxes, and homeowners insurance. Moreover, lenders will usually turn you down if more than 36 percent of your gross income goes to paying all your long-term debts, including the mortgage and such obligations as alimony, car payments, and longstanding credit-card balances. Thus, if you wanted to buy a $100,000 house and borrow $80,000 at a fixed rate of 12½ percent, your annual income would have to be more than $43,000. But to qualify for an $80,000 adjustable-rate loan at 10 percent, you would need to earn only $36,500.

Assuming you have a choice, how do you decide between a fixed-rate loan at 12½ percent and an ARM that starts at 10 percent? For an answer, take a look at both types of mortgage and the home buyers for whom each is best suited:

FIXED-RATE LOANS

In summer 1984, conventional 30-year mortgages looked like a thing of the past. Interest rates were at 14 percent to 15 percent, and some lenders were offering adjustable loans with initial interest rates, called teaser rates, as low as 7½ percent. As a result, ARMs accounted for two-thirds of the mortgages being made. Now that interest rates have declined by almost two percentage points, home buyers are flocking back to fixed rates. Says Patric Hendershott, a professor of real estate at Ohio State University: "The spread between fixed rates and ARMs got as high as 2¾ percentage points, but now it tends to be around 2¼ points." When the difference between fixed and variable rates is two percentage points or less, borrowers begin to ignore ARMs. By the first of 1985, more than half of all new mortgages carried fixed rates.

If you can borrow at a fixed rate, you should do so. Housing economists believe that mortgage rates may have hit bottom at about 11 percent at year end. Should rates decline still more, you can refinance your loan by paying off the mortgage and taking out a new one. As a rule, rates have to drop two to three percentage points below yours for refinancing to be worthwhile, since you will have to pay closing costs and perhaps an early-payment penalty.

The virtue of a fixed-rate loan is just that—your mortgage costs are fixed. Such a loan is ideal for a young couple who are anticipating starting a family. They need to know what their monthly mortgage bill is going to be, particularly if one spouse's income might disappear with the arrival of children.

Not everyone who wants predictable housing expenses needs a 30-year loan, however. Shorter term variations on the traditional fixed-rate mortgage—especially a 15-year version—are being aggressively marketed by lenders. Nervous about making long-term commitments, bankers are enhancing the appeal of these loans by charging lower rates for them than they do for 30-year mortgages. The spread is typically one-quarter to one-half a percentage point. Monthly payments on an $80,000 loan at 12¾ percent, a typical rate for 15 years, would be $999.07 vs. $884.96 for 30 years at 13 percent. In exchange for the higher monthly payments, a borrower could save as much as $138,753 in interest costs by paying off the mortgage much faster. Most people don't live in the same house long enough to repay their mortgages; in fact, a typical house is resold about every seven years. Even so, a 15-year borrower almost always comes out ahead of one whose loan runs 30 years, because he builds up more equity by the time he sells. For this reason, a professional couple reasonably confident of a rising income might find a 15-year loan appealing. They'd wind up with more money for the down payment on their next house.

If you are an executive who is regularly bounced from place to place by a company, you could gamble on yet another variation of the fixed-rate mortgage—a three-year balloon loan. Since the term is so short, you should be able to negotiate a reduction of one to two percentage points from the normal rate for 30-year fixed-rate mortgages. The advantage of a balloon loan is that for three years you might lock in a lower rate than you would get with an adjustable loan. The drawback is that if you don't sell your house before the three years are up, you'll have to refinance your mortgage. Your lender will charge one to three points for that, and by then mortgage rates could be vying with the Voyager spacecraft to see who blasts out of the solar system first. Says Barry Havemann, president of HSH Associates of Riverdale, New Jersey, a mortgage consulting firm: "Smaller banks are the most likely to give you this kind of deal. It's used so frequently in financing small businesses that it's a familiar, comfortable product to them."

ADJUSTABLE-RATE LOANS

These days both borrowers and lenders are taking a more cautious attitude toward variable-rate mortgages. Some homeowners, reeling from the shock of rising payments combined with stagnating property values, have begun to default on their loans, and foreclosures are at their highest levels since the recession of 1973-75. Mortgage insurance companies are belatedly protecting themselves by insisting that bankers set stiffer requirements to screen borrowers for adjustable-rate mortgages. Lenders now must qualify home buyers based on a realistic interest rate, usually around 10 percent, rather than some artificially low introductory rate. As a result, teaser rates have all but disappeared.

The best candidate for an ARM is someone whose income is likely to increase substantially. An ARM loses its menace if you can outrun the increases in payments. A doctor or lawyer just beginning to practice, or a young corporate executive, might not be able to afford a home with a fixed-rate loan at 12 percent or 13 percent, but may be able to handle payments on the same size loan at an initial rate of 10 percent.

ARMs can be attractive for someone who reckons that interest rates will fall. But even if rates should go up, a young homeowner with a rising income will still be better off with a variable-rate loan as long as he is certain of moving within a couple of years and the mortgage contains no prepayment penalty. For example, you would pay $702.06 a month for an $80,000 adjustable loan at 10 percent vs. $822.90 at a fixed rate of 12 percent. At the end of the first year, you would have saved $1,450.08 with an ARM, and chances are you'd be slightly ahead in your second year despite the increase in your payments. Since adjustable-rate loans are generally assumable by another buyer, whereas fixed-rate loans usually are not, your ARM could make your house easier to sell.

After an initial period, your mortgage payments on an ARM will go up or down based on two factors: the index to which the loan is tied and the lending institution's profit margin. So the introductory rate is less critical than the basis for future adjustments.

Lenders peg adjustable loans to a variety of indexes, but by far the most common ones are based on Treasury securities. For example, an ARM tied to the six-month T-bill rate would be adjusted on the six-month anniversary of your loan and every six months thereafter in line with the current T-bill rate. A loan linked to the one-year Treasury-security rate would change annually with the one-year rate prevailing on the anniversary of your loan. Interest-rate fluctuations between your adjustments do not affect what you pay.

Treasury indexes are comparatively volatile, an advantage to borrowers when interest rates are dropping but not when they are rising. A more sluggish index is the Federal Home Loan Bank Board's average contract rate on fixed-rate and variable mortgages recently issued by major lenders. Borrowers get good protection against rate increases, but the index is likely to linger in the stratosphere when rates are declining. The bank board's median cost-of-funds index "is safer for the consumer," says David E. Sharp, chairman of Home Federal Savings Bank of Tennessee in Knoxville. "It's not as volatile as a Treasury index and it's more current than the average mortgage rate." The cost of funds is the interest lenders pay on the money they get from depositors.

Of course, few lenders let you select an index, but you should make sure you know which one your mortgage will be tied to. If you can't get a satisfactory explanation of how the changes in the index will affect your loan, take your business elsewhere. For example, state-chartered banks and savings and loans in a few places create indexes based on their own cost of funds. Since that information is not available to the public, an index based on it is open to manipulation. Steer clear of loans linked to such indexes and of the lenders who offer them. (The table on page 41 shows how the same loan tied to the one-year Treasury-security rate, the Federal Home Loan Bank Board's average mortgage contract rate, and the bank board's median cost-of-funds index would have varied over the past five years.)

Changes in the index account for only part of each adjustment to your mortgage. To any increase—or decrease—in the index, lenders add their profit margin, which is typically 2 percent to 2½ percent of the loan. Here's how this works: Say a year ago you financed your house with a one-year ARM at an initial rate of 10 percent, tied to the one-year Treasury-security rate. Your lender's margin is 2½ percent. Now it's time for your adjustment, and the Treasury rate is 9 percent. Presto! You have an 11½ percent loan.

Neither you as a borrower nor your bank or savings and loan as a lender want you to be completely at the mercy of interest-rate fluctuations. No one comes out ahead, including the lender, if you are so impoverished by untethered gyrations that you can't make your payments. That's why more than three-quarters of all new ARMs have limits, called caps, on the amount of each adjustment and on total increases in the rate during the life of your loan. Usually the caps are one to two percentage points a year and five points over the life of the loan.

Two types of cap are treacherous, however. Watch out for one that limits increases in your payments while the interest rate on the mortgage is allowed to bob up and down. The result could be a loan that is growing instead of diminishing as you make payments. Reason: whenever you are not paying the full cost of the loan, because you aren't paying all the interest you owe, the excess gets added to your loan balance.

Be wary also of a cap that doesn't take effect with the first rate adjustment. Some loans, especially those with unusually low teaser rates, are advanced to the full index plus the lender's profit margin at the time of the first adjustment and capped thereafter. Before you accept such a loan, advises Jane Greenstein, president of Mortgage Clearing House Inc., a mortgage advisory service for home buyers, in New Hyde Park, New York, "make sure your current income is sufficient to handle the highest possible second-year payments."

When you are shopping for your mortgage, start with the lender where you already have a checking or savings account or a personal loan. You have the advantage of being a known risk. If you can't get the loan you want there, begin comparison shopping among local lenders. Concentrate on mortgage bankers for a fixed-rate loan, savings and loans for an ARM. In your search you may also encounter mortgage brokers, small outfits that charge a fee to find money for you. Some can be helpful in locating a good deal, but since mortgage funds are plentiful, you're not likely to need a middleman.

Armed with information about loans, you can mount your own search for funds. But rare is the shopper who self-confidently confronts lenders on their own territory. Some helpful allies are firms that survey the marketplace, then publish their findings as to rates, terms, and costs. Each week HSH Associates (10 Mead Ave., Riverdale, N.J. 07457) compiles mortgage data from lenders in parts of California, Connecticut, Florida, New Jersey, and New York. The cost is $10 a copy. The Peeke Report (101 Chestnut St., Gaithersburg, Md. 20877; $15 a copy) covers Washington, D.C., plus sections of Florida, Maryland, and Virginia. A number of other companies have computer networks that advertise the wares of participating mortgage lenders (see the following box). Finally, don't overlook your real estate agent. Says Russell Rothstein, assistant vice president of Investors Home Mortgage Corp. in Rockville, Maryland: "A broker will know who delivers loans as promised." Fine—as long as you understand what's being promised.

MORTGAGE SHOPPING BY COMPUTER

The promise is tantalizing: instead of trekking around town in search of a mortgage, you can arrange for one without ever leaving your real estate agent's office. He punches a few keys on a desktop computer and up pops the most attractive available loan. This is known as computerized mortgage origination. In some cases, the computer cannot only sort through various types of loans to come up with the best rate and terms for which you would qualify but also accept your application, give you a conditional commitment subject to a credit check, and process the loan.

The convenience of borrowing by computer is very appealing, and the number of companies offering the service is steadily increasing. But does electronic mortgage

shopping live up to its promise? For now, the answer is
maybe. The computer can uncover attractive rates, but you
may be able to do better on your own.

A *Money Guide* reporter compared the terms of loans
offered by traditional lenders with those of two firms spe-
cializing in computerized mortgage origination in the
Baltimore-Washington, D.C., area. The goal was to find the
best $80,000 mortgage on a hypothetical $100,000 house.
The two firms were Mortgage Resources Corp. in Towson,
Maryland, and PRC LoanExpress in Falls Church, Virginia. Mortgage Resources, a subsidiary of O'Conor Piper
& Flynn Realtors, is among 1,500 real estate brokers and
mortgage companies nationwide that use Shelternet, by far
the largest of the half-dozen national loan origination programs. PRC uses its own computer system that links 40
lenders with 300 real estate offices in metropolitan Washington, D.C.

After their computers digested an application that
reported an income of $50,000 and savings of $25,000, the
two firms' printers spit out long lists of possible mortgages.
Neither concern would divulge the names of the lenders.
PRC frets that borrowers would go directly to the lender
offering the best deal, thus evading the firm's origination
fee of 1 percent of the mortgage amount. So PRC waits until
the loan application has been submitted before telling customers who the lender is. Customers are also charged
$27.50 for a credit report and a $150 for an appraisal. Shelternet's funds come mostly from savings and loan
associations, and borrowers learn the identity of their lender
at closing. Shelternet's fees run about $200.

Money Guide looked at the terms on a one-year adjustable-rate loan and a 30-year fixed-rate loan. The computer-
originated loans were compared with those offered by traditional lenders as surveyed by the Peeke Report for the week
of January 21, 1985. Both PRC loans were competitive in the
metropolitan Washington, D.C., area, as was Shelternet's
fixed-rate loan in Baltimore. However, Shelternet's ARM
terms did not match those of local lending institutions or PRC.

Shelternet's ARM, an atypical 29-year loan, carried an
initial rate of 10 percent, plus points equaling $3\frac{3}{4}$ percent of
the loan amount, or $3,000. There were caps on future rate
increases of two points a year and five points over the life of
the loan and a profit margin for the lender of $2\frac{3}{4}$ percent of

Financing

the loan amount. Monthly payments in the first year: $735.47. In Baltimore, about half the lenders offered better rates and lower points. Most had lower profit margins too.

A PRC customer could get an ARM package consisting of a 9½ percent first-year rate, four points, or $3,200, caps of two points a year and 4 points over the life of the loan, and a 2½ percent profit margin. Monthly payments: $672.68. By shopping diligently among local lenders, you could have found more favorable terms at Dominion Mortgage Funding in McLean, Virginia. Seven other lenders listed in the Peeke Report had loans with terms as good as PRC's or better.

For a 30-year fixed-rate mortgage, Shelternet offered 12¾ percent plus 2¾ points, or $2,200. Monthly payments: $869.35. Four of 80 Baltimore lenders had better deals. For example, Germania Federal offered a 12½ percent loan, with 2½ points, or $2,000. PRC weighed in with a 12½ percent mortgage rate but with four points, or $3,200. Monthly payments for both were $853.82. In metropolitan Washington, there were no better rates offered. Seven of 62 firms did have fewer points.

The moral: touch as many bases as possible when looking for the best mortgage rate.

—Lionel C. Bascom

HOW PAYMENTS VARY

If you have an adjustable rate mortgage, your interest rate
and monthly payments vary with movements in the index to
which the mortgage is tied. The table at left shows how the
payments on an $80,000 loan would have fluctuated over
five years in line with three common indexes described in
the accompanying story. The rates include lenders' profit
margins of up to 2½ percent of the loan principal.

Your mortgage costs over the past five years would have
been lowest with the cost-of-funds index—$55,616.40—and
highest if linked to the Treasury-security rate—$65,942.30.
Of course, these results would have been different if interest
rates had been less erratic.

INTEREST RATES

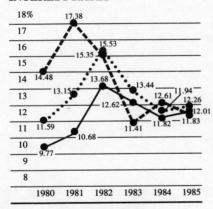

MONTHLY PAYMENTS

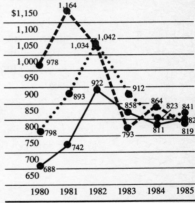

——— **Cost-of-funds index**   ▬ ▬ ▬ ▬ **One-Year Treasury securities**
•••••• **Mortgage contract rate**

Checklist
Fixed-rate mortgages are best if . . .

☐ Your income is fairly stable and you want housing costs that are predictable.

☐ You can afford to pay 12½ percent to 13 percent interest, plus fees equal to 1 percent to 4 percent of your loan amount.

☐ You don't plan to move for at least five years.

Consider an adjustable-rate loan if . . .

☐ You can't qualify for a fixed-rate loan at current interest rates.

☐ Your income is steadily rising and you can outrun any increases in your payments.

☐ You don't expect to be in your house for more than a couple of years.

☐ The interest rate on your loan is attached to a stable index, such as the Federal Home Loan Bank Board's median cost of funds or the bank board's contract mortgage rate.

☐ Your lender's profit is no more than 2½ percentage points above the index he uses.

☐ The mortgage has caps on how much and how often the interest rate can be adjusted—but not on your monthly payments.

The Unexpected Costs of Buying a Home

Robert Runde

Behind the down payment and the mortgage lurk a number of nettlesome expenses.

When you buy a house, you'll discover there is a lot more to the price than what the seller is asking for. As a rule, buyers wind up spending an additional 5 percent to 8 percent of the amount of their mortgage on what are commonly known as closing or settlement costs. The closing is the meeting between buyer and seller at which the property legally changes hands. Three days after you apply for a mortgage, your lender must send you a detailed estimate of the costs you will face at closing. Among the extras you're most likely to encounter:

► Loan application fees. Many lenders insist that you pay $75 to $300 simply to apply for a mortage. The money is intended to cover the costs of processing your application, obtaining a credit report, and, in some cases, appraising the property. If there is no application fee, you may be billed separately for an appraisal ($150 to $300) and a credit report ($30 to $75).

► Loan origination fees. Most banks and savings and loans charge 1 percent of your mortgage amount to cover their overhead in processing your loan, a complicated procedure that usually takes two to four weeks. You may have to come

43

up with the money for this fee at the time you receive your mortgage commitment.

▶ Points. Once you have taken care of your lender's overhead with loan application and origination fees, you are usually required to make an upfront payment to assure him of part of his profit and protect him against rising interest rates. This tariff, which you pay at the closing, is calculated in units called points, with each point equaling 1 percent of your mortgage. You should expect to pay one to four points. You can also use points to buy down your interest rate. On a 30-year mortgage, each extra point you pay reduces your rate by about one-sixth of 1 percent. For example, by paying $2,400—three points—on an $80,000 loan, you could reduce the rate from 12½ percent to 12 percent.

▶ Mortgage insurance. A loan officer's best protection against having to foreclose on your house is your investment in it. Buyers who can't put down at least 20 percent of the purchase price are required by most lenders, and by law in some states, to buy private mortgage insurance to cover the lender's risk above 80 percent of the price of the house. You'll be charged a one-time fee of half a point—that's half of 1 percent of your mortgage—to one point, plus annual premiums of one-quarter to three-eighths of a point until the loan principal is less than 75 percent of the value of the house. You're likely to keep paying those premiums for 10 years or more unless your house is appreciating fairly rapidly. In that case, have your house reappraised and you may be able to persuade the lender to drop the mortgage insurance requirement after two or three years.

▶ Title search and insurance fees. Mortgage lenders want proof that the seller has a clear title to the property you are buying, so they bill you for the cost of a title search. You are also required to buy insurance to cover the possibility that the researcher missed something. In Virginia, for example, on a $100,000 house with an $80,000 mortgage, the two fees would total about $260.

▶ Attorneys' fees. In some states, a title company or an escrow firm will handle the closing. For instance, in California, an escrow company does all the work for $150. There are attorneys who specialize in real estate settlements and who represent all parties at the closing; in Virginia, for example, they typically charge you a fee of about $225 to attend to the settlement. Elsewhere, you may need to hire your own lawyer. In many places, two or even three lawyers are present at the closing, representing the buyer, the seller, and the lender. The buyer's attorney does most of the work and usually charges $500 to $1,000. Even so, in such states as New Jersey, the lender may still bill a buyer $300 to $400 for the time its lawyer spends preparing the loan documents.

► Adjustments. If the bank pays your property taxes as part of servicing your mortgage, you'll be charged a fraction of the next tax bill at settlement and every time you make a mortgage payment. This way the lender gradually accumulates a fund from which to pay the taxes. In most cases, the seller will already have paid a portion of the forthcoming tax bill. You'll have to reimburse him for the part of his payment that covers the time when you own the property. You're also obligated to compensate the seller for whatever heating oil remains in the tank when you take the house over, any dues he prepaid to a condominium or property owners' association, and any fixtures you've agreed to buy from him. If you didn't settle up with him earlier, the $100 you're giving him for that birdbath in the backyard will appear as an adjustment at the closing.

► Homeowners insurance. It's up to you to insure the house, but at the closing you must show that you have a policy, with the first year's premium already paid. The premium can vary widely, but it is likely to be in the range of $300 to $600 a year for a single-family house and somewhat less for a condominium (see "Guarding Your Castle Against Calamity," next chapter).

► Home inspection. This is an optional expense, but you would be foolish not to pay a professional building inspector to make sure the house is sound. An inspection can cost $150 to $300, which you pay the professional at the time he makes his examination. Pest inspections are routinely required before a house changes hands. However, the seller frequently pays that bill, typically $25 to $50.

► Taxes. Your local government—community, county, or state—may muscle in on the closing, demanding its due. The sum can be burdensome. A home buyer in Montgomery County, Maryland, for example, must pay a state transfer tax of one-half of 1 percent of the selling price plus a county transfer tax of up to 1 percent. Then the state requires him to buy tax stamps, at $4.40 per $1,000 of the house price. On a $100,000 house, a buyer would be skinned for $1,940. In

Pennsylvania, the state levies a 1 percent tax and the municipality adds another 1 percent. So taxes on a $100,000 house would be $2,000, but buyer and seller usually split the expense. There are no transfer taxes at all in some states, California and Texas among them. Other states may levy a tax based on the size of a mortgage.

Just when you think you've paid every conceivable title, tariff, and tax, a few more bills crop up to annoy you. The lender usually requires a survey of the property, and that can cost $125 to $300. Then, in places where you don't use your own attorney, there's apt to be a $10 to $25 charge for the notary who witnesses your signature on the various documents. But you'll know you've finally reached the end of the line when you have paid $40 to $60 to have your deed recorded.

WHEN MORE IS LESS

Many of the extra expenses of home buying protect the lender against having to foreclose on your house, a time-consuming and expensive procedure. The more money you have in your home, the more confident a loan officer is that you will not default on your mortgage. So if your down payment is substantial, you can forgo mortgage insurance. Moreover, some of your fees and taxes will be lower. Advises Robert Potash, a real estate lawyer in Greenwich, Connecticut: "Make a down payment of 20 percent whenever possible. That alone can trim hundreds or even thousands of dollars off your closing costs."

No two transactions will have exactly the same fees, but here is a typical example of the differences in closing costs between a 20 percent down payment and one of 10 percent on a $100,000 house in New York State:

DOWN PAYMENT	20 PERCENT	10 PERCENT
Loan application fee	$100 to $300	$100 to $300
Loan origination fee	800	900
Points	800 to 2,400	900 to 2,700
Mortgage insurance	—	450 to 900
Title search and insurance	485	525
Attorneys' fees	500 to 1,500	500 to 1,500
Homeowners insurance	500	500
Home inspection	150 to 300	150 to 300
Mortgage tax	575	650
Survey	125 to 300	125 to 300
Recording fee	40 to 60	40 to 60
TOTAL	$4,075 to $7,220	$4,840 to $8,635

Financing

Where to Find a Down Payment

Robert Runde

With the 5 percent solution,
buying a house may be easier
than you think.

The biggest hurdle facing you as a first-time home buyer
is not finding a house you can afford. It's coming up
with the cash to make the down payment on a house you can
just barely afford. A surprisingly available option: the 5 percent solution.

Lenders prefer that you make a big down payment; your
substantial investment in the house reassures them that you
will not default on your mortgage (see "The Unexpected
Costs of Buying a Home," page 43). But you shouldn't automatically assume you have to raise 10 percent or 20 percent of
the purchase price in cash. It is possible to buy a home with
little or nothing down.

The easiest terms come with a mortgage backed by the
Veterans Administration. If you have served in the armed
forces, you may be able to get a loan for 100 percent of the
cost of the house. You apply for a VA-guaranteed loan at
banks, mortgage companies, and some savings and loans just
as you would for any other type of mortgage. You must borrow the money at a fixed rate, roughly the market rate. When
the VA rate is below the market rate, however, a lender will
demand extra points. The buyer is allowed to pay just one
point, so the seller has to pick up the rest.

You don't have to be a veteran to qualify for the Federal
Housing Administration's mortgage program. An FHA-

insured loan, which you apply for through a conventional lender, can cover up to 95 percent of the entire outlay—including closing costs—for a house. And you may find an FHA-backed adjustable-rate mortgage with interest and points that are slightly better than you'd get on other ARMs. FHA mortgages have ceilings set by law, however. In most places, you can't borrow more than $67,500, although in such high-cost metropolitan areas as Minneapolis and San Diego the maximum is $90,000.

You can also get a 95 percent loan without government backing. Many lenders will write you a mortgage for that much as long as your income is high enough to meet the payments and your credit rating is impeccable. Closing costs would be higher than they would be for comparable VA and FHA loans, which can include those expenses and mortgage insurance as part of the mortgage principal. Thus you would have to come up with a wad of cash that could equal or even be slightly more than the down payment if your loan is not insured by the government.

When you are making a minimal down payment while applying for a maximum mortgage, the lender will scrutinize your credit history closely. Says Jane Greenstein, president of Mortgage Clearing House Inc., an advisory service for borrowers, in New Hyde Park, New York: "A good record on auto and student loans is important. If you are constantly late with your payments, that looks bad. If you haven't begun repaying a student loan that's due, you'll give a lender the idea you're trying to stiff the government."

Once you know that you can qualify for 95 percent financing, you can start hunting for the cash to cover both the down payment and closing costs. Examine your own assets first. You're not likely to have a sizable portfolio of stocks and bonds, but you might have an Individual Retirement Account. You'll pay ordinary income tax on the money you withdraw early from an IRA as well as a 10 percent penalty, but those costs may be outweighed by the tax deductions the house will generate. It is possible that the deduction for mortgage interest and property taxes will wipe out the tax levies on the IRA withdrawal. Advises Don Zoch, a Fairfield, New Jersey, financial planner: "Be cautious about spending your IRA, but if you must, buy a house early in the year to get the maximum tax benefits from it."

Corporate thrift plans—profit-sharing programs and

401(k) salary-reduction plans—are another resource. When you borrow from them, you can expect to be charged an interest rate somewhat lower than you'd pay at a bank. The typical range recently was 9½ percent to 11½ percent. In plans that allow loans, you can borrow $10,000 or half the balance in your account, up to a maximum of $50,000 without any tax consequences.

The advantage of borrowing your down payment from a corporate plan is that the loan probably will not show up on any credit rating. Your company is unlikely to report it because you are borrowing your own money. Lenders look at the size of your long-term debts as reported by a credit bureau to figure out if you can afford the mortgage you want. They'll usually refuse your application if more than 36 percent of your income is going to debt repayments, including the mortgage.

After you have exhausted your own resources, you will probably turn to your family for help, as many first-time buyers do. Even if you have every intention of repaying your folks, you may have to give the lender a letter from the family stating that the money is a gift, not a loan.

Lenders are more likely to qualify you for a mortgage if some of your own money, as opposed to borrowed cash, is invested in the house. They reckon your equity will be a powerful incentive for you to keep up your payments.

One person can give another as much as $10,000 a year without either of them having to pay gift taxes. So a husband and wife could bestow a tax-free $40,000 on a married child and spouse. Parents can also make interest-free or low-interest loans to their children of up to $100,000 to help them buy a house, as long as the child's net investment income is less than $1,000. Otherwise the parents may have to pay taxes on the interest their loan ought to be generating. The IRS sets the appropriate rate of interest every six months, based on the yield for short-term Treasury securities.

Rather than ask your parents for the down payment, you could suggest that they become co-owners of the house with you in return for making the down payment and paying some or all of the closing costs. That way you could buy a more expensive home than you could on your own and your parents could qualify for significant tax breaks. Consider, for example, Craig S. Smith, an endocrinologist, and his wife Terri, who earlier this year bought a $150,000 house in Car-michael, California, a suburb of Sacramento. Having recently purchased a partnership in a private clinic, Dr. Smith, 33, was short of cash, so his father agreed to chip in half the down payment and closing costs in return for becoming a half-owner of the house. For a fee of $1,979.50—$250 plus 1 percent of the mortgage amount—Family-Backed Mortgage Association (2585 Ordway Bldg., 1 Kaiser Plaza, Oakland, Calif. 94612), a company that specializes in shared ownerships, worked out all the details of the transaction.

If you are contemplating a shared-ownership arrangement with your parents or someone else, you may want to consider hiring a firm to help you with the paperwork. These deals are complex because parents in effect become landlords and their children tenants. They split the expenses of owning the house, but in order for the parents to take depreciation and the other tax deductions available to owners of income property, the children have to pay rent at what the IRS will accept as a fair market rate. In the Smiths' case, this was $381 a month.

The seller of the house you want to buy can be the source of the down payment. You are most likely to get his help when interest rates are rising and he is having difficulty unloading his property. But even when rates are dropping, a seller may be receptive to an unconventional arrangement. Says Andrew C. Levine, a New York City real estate lawyer: "If the seller doesn't need the cash right away, you may be able to negotiate terms that are better for both of you."

One possibility is a lease agreement with an option to buy, which lets you test-drive a house or condo without making an irrevocable commitment. If you decide not to buy, you won't be out too much money. In 1982, Miriam Lippman, a junior high school guidance counselor, decided to move to a one-bedroom condo in Silver Spring, Maryland. She signed a rental agreement with an option to buy the place at the end of one year. Her monthly payment was $600, of which $200 went toward an eventual down payment. A year later, when she exercised her option on the $90,000 condo, she had saved up $2,400 of the down payment. She would have forfeited it if she had decided not to buy.

You may be able to work out a non-cash down payment with the seller. If the house is dilapidated, you might offer to make needed repairs or improvements in lieu of part or all of the down payment. The advantage of this arrangement for the seller is that should you later default on your loan, he can foreclose on a property that is more salable than it was before you bought it. Real estate consultant Donna Milling of Data Mill Inc., in Thornton, Pennsylvania, recommends that you "talk with the seller at length to find out what his real needs are. All sellers think they must have cash, but some would rather just be rid of the property."

Reporter associate: Martha Mader

Financing

Checklist

The more money you can put down on a house, the better off you are—at least over the long run. But if you are struggling to come up with even a modest down payment, you can still buy a house. The resources you might be overlooking include:

☐ Government-backed VA and FHA mortgages.

☐ Your Individual Retirement Account.

☐ Your company's thrift plans, including profit-sharing and 401(k) salary-reduction programs.

☐ Your parents, who can give you and your spouse up to $40,000 tax-free; they can also become co-owners of your house.

☐ The seller, who can let you rent the house with an option to buy it to help you build a down payment. He may even agree not to demand a cash down payment if you are willing to improve the property.

Guarding Your Castle Against Calamity

Walter L. Updegrave

Homeowners insurance covers
your house and its contents, but
how much is enough?

Ever since the Phoenix, England's first fire insurance
company, began insuring private houses after the Great
Fire of London in 1666, homeowners have grappled with the
problem of protecting their property against disaster without
causing one in the family budget. While a 17th-century
Londoner could buy coverage strictly limited to fire damage
to the structure of his home, today's homeowner can insure
not only the structure but also its contents against fire, theft,
and a wide range of other disasters. In addition, homeowners
insurance includes personal-liability protection for injuries
visitors sustain on your premises and for damage you may do
to the property of others. But this extra protection doesn't
come cheap. On average, policyholders pay $249 annually to
guard their dwellings against catastrophe.

Homeowners insurance ranges from basic stripped-down
policies that safeguard your castle only from named perils
such as fire, windstorm, and hail to so-called all-risk coverage that will reimburse you should your water pipes burst or
your roof collapse. Whatever standard policy you buy must
then be tailored to your specific needs with a series of riders

called endorsements. These endorsements invariably boost your premiums.

Last year, the Insurance Services Office (ISO), a trade organization that provides most of the standard policy forms used by the insurance industry, introduced a new home-owners contract that should alleviate some of the worry about how much protection is enough. Called Homeowners Program, this policy raises the deductible—the portion of the loss that you pay before your insurance kicks in—from the now standard $100 to $250. But it also provides more personal-liability protection and better coverage for such possessions as jewelry, furs, and computers used at home for business purposes. This basic policy will cost about the same as existing ones. Since ISO policies usually become the industry standard, the new Homeowners Program, currently approved in eight states, should be available nationwide by 1986.

When you shop for insurance, don't be lulled into a false sense of security by the term all risk. Even the most comprehensive policies—Homeowners Program included—have exclusions. They don't cover losses caused by war, nuclear accident, earthquake, or, to the surprise of irate victims, flood.

The amount of homeowners insurance you should carry depends on the replacement cost of your house—what you would have to spend to rebuild your manse as it now stands. Don't confuse this concept with market value or you could wind up seriously over- or under-insuring your dwelling. The replacement cost for a newly constructed home, for example, is typically only 75 percent of the purchase price. The land and the foundation are virtually indestructible and generally are not insured. Conversely, the replacement cost of a Victorian townhouse, say, with carved mahogany banisters and ornate gingerbread woodwork can outstrip what the house would fetch if resold.

Most insurance companies figure out replacement value by using cost-estimating forms. They consider such factors as the soundness of construction, the number of rooms, and the quality of kitchen appliances and bathroom fixtures. This method is fine for the typical house, but if you own a custom-designed or period home, you should get a written estimate of its replacement cost from a real estate appraiser.

Insurance companies prefer that you insure your home for 100 percent of replacement cost, but total losses are rare and you'll be adequately covered for partial damage with 80 percent. Reducing your coverage from 100 percent of replacement value to 80 percent can lower premium costs by as much as 20 percent.

You should make sure your policy indexes the replacement costs to inflation. Sluggish real estate values of recent years might tempt you to forgo this extra protection, but that would be a big mistake. Replacement costs move independent of a home's market value. During the past two years, residential construction costs have climbed 9.8 percent, while the resale price of homes has risen 7.2 percent. For this reason, if you make a substantial improvement to your home, raise your coverage to reflect the new replacement cost.

All homeowners policies cover your personal possessions—from rugs, furniture, and appliances to art, jewelry, furs, and the family silver. But important limits apply here. Most contracts, including the new Homeowners Program, restrict the total claim for personal possessions to 50 percent of the amount of coverage on the house itself. Insure your home for $90,000 and the most you can collect on the contents is $45,000. Moreover, you are reimbursed not for a destroyed item's replacement cost but for its actual cash value—replacement cost minus depreciation. So that five-year-old TV that went up in smoke might fetch only $100 instead of the $700 you paid for it or the $600 it would cost to replace it today.

To make sure that you'll be adequately reimbursed when you make a claim, add a replacement-cost endorsement for personal contents to your policy. Your yearly premium will go up 10 percent to 15 percent, but the extra protection is worth it. And to have enough coverage for a major disaster, raise the claim limit from 50 percent to 70 percent. The cost: about $1 per additional $1,000 in coverage.

A replacement-cost endorsement for personal contents is especially important for condominium owners. The condo association insures the structural elements, so an owner is in effect buying only the personal contents portion of a homeowners policy. If you own a condo, you should bear in mind that the association's insurance doesn't cover interior structural improvements. So if you renovate the kitchen or redo the bathroom, be sure to add replacement-value coverage under the additions and alterations or betterments and improvements section of the policy.

Financing

A much lower reimbursement limit than actual cash value applies to jewelry, furs, silverware, and collectibles. If a thief makes off with your $5,000 diamond bracelet, the standard policy pays you only $500. The new Homeowners Program policy raises the coverages on jewelry, furs, and negotiable securities to $1,000 and on gold and silverware to $2,500. A blanket endorsement can boost your protection up to a maximum of $10,000 for about $3 per $100 value of jewelry, $1 per $100 for furs, and 25¢ per $100 for fine art. Blanket coverage, however, may still have a limit for individual items. Therefore valuables worth more than $2,500 should be itemized and insured individually. To support a claim, you'll need sales receipts and appraisals for all valuables that are covered by endorsements.

Many older homeowners policies still have only $25,000 in liability coverage, although the Homeowners Program offers $100,000. Even that might not be enough. Jury Verdict Research, a Solon, Ohio, firm that keeps records of jury awards in personal-injury cases, reports that the average payment for spinal fractures is $138,320. The probability of being hit with a judgment of that size is remote, but extra protection costs so little it's foolish not to have it. Raising your coverage to $100,000 adds an extra $10 a year to your premium, and $500,000 worth of protection costs $30. For less than $100 a year, you can buy $1 million in excess liability coverage, which pays claims above the limits on both your homeowners and auto policies.

Homeowners policies don't usually cover commercial activities, so if you work part-time out of your house, add an incidental business option to your policy. With it, you can insure up to $10,000 of business property for about $20 a year and extend your liability protection to the business. Many newer policies such as Homeowners Program automatically cover up to $2,500 worth of business equipment used at home. But if your residence is also your primary place of business, you'll probably need the more expensive but more comprehensive Business Owners Policy. Premiums start at $200 to $250 for $20,000 of property protection and $500,000 worth of liability insurance.

By the time you are through shaping your homeowners policy to your particular circumstances, you'll discover that the premiums add up. One way to hold them down is to take advantage of the special deals offered by most insurers. If your house was built within the past two years, you're eligible for a 20 percent new-home discount. The discount diminishes by three percentage points every two years, so a four-year-old house rates a 14 percent reduction in premium and a 10-year-old dwelling qualifies for 8 percent. Installing dead bolts and smoke detectors in your home can knock 5 percent off your annual premium cost. A sophisticated home-protection system—fire and burglar alarms that report to a central station—will lower your outlay 20 percent a year. The discounts are also cumulative. "If you have a new home with a central station alarm," says Bonnie McHenry, a homeowners insurance specialist at Aetna Life & Casualty, "you can save up to 40 percent."

Increase your deductible and you will also decrease your premium. Agree to absorb the first $250 of any loss instead of the standard $100 and you lop 10 percent off your annual bill. Jump to a $500 deductible and you take off as much as 20 percent. If your budget can handle a $1,000 loss, you can pocket savings of up to 25 percent, and those whose finances are solid enough to absorb $2,500 or $5,000 hits can reduce premiums 30 percent and 35 percent respectively.

But don't let the quest for savings lead you into the trap of choosing a low deductible and scrimping on the overall coverage to cut your premium. Countless homeowners, too concerned about getting reimbursed for minor losses, have given in to this temptation, leaving themselves dangerously underinsured against major risks. "Insurance is really there for the catastrophic situation," says Richard Simpson, homeowners insurance underwriter for the Hartford Insurance Group. "If you need to keep the cost down, do it with the deductible, not with the amount of coverage.

WARRANTIES FOR NEW HOUSES

You have been living in your *palazzo* for two months when the foundation starts to shift, causing the rafters to crack and the walls to buckle. What are you going to do? Your homeowners policy covers you for fires and force-10 gales but not for structural flaws. If yours is a new house, chances are that it came with a builder warranty—a protection plan that, in effect, insures the dwelling against defects in the structure as well as in the plumbing, electrical, heating, and cooling systems. Many home builders provide one-year warranties, but you are much better off with one of the 10-year plans offered through builders by independent warranty companies such as Builders Trust Warranty in Pompano Beach, Florida, Home Buyers Warranty in Denver, and Home Owners Warranty in Washington, D.C. The builder pays the one-time premium, which is usually $2 to $2.50 per $1,000 of the sales price.

Home Owners Warranty (HOW) is by far the largest writer of warranties for new houses, and its plan is typical of the way most work. For the first two years, the warranty covers major structural problems as well as deficiencies in wiring, piping, and ductwork. The homeowner takes his complaints directly to the builder, who is responsible for correcting them. In the warranty's third through 10th years, only major structural defects are covered, and homeowners must direct their complaints to HOW, which will arrange for a contractor to fix the problem.

If during the first two years the builder and homeowner disagree about whether a problem is covered by the warranty or how a defect should be fixed, HOW summons an arbitrator to decide who is responsible for repairs. The builder must comply with that decision. If the homeowner is not satisfied, he has the right to sue the builder and HOW for repairs that weren't made. This right extends even to homeowners with more than one claim for damage who accept the settlement in order to get some of the work done.

HOW also offers a five-year warranty for remodeled homes that covers structural defects in the renovated sections and, for the first two years, problems with wiring, piping, and ductwork that have been replaced or altered. But the remodeling warranty, introduced two years ago, has yet to catch on the way the new-home program has.

Warranties are also available for existing homes through independent warranty companies and real estate chains such as ERA and Century 21. But in most cases, these warranties are designed to insure homes only at the time of sale. If you are selling your house, you can cover it during the listing period and up to a year after it is sold. Home buyers can also purchase coverage that protects the house for a year after closing. A few companies let you renew the warranty annually.

The plans for existing homes don't guarantee you against structural problems, but they do protect you against wear and tear specifically excluded in homeowners insurance contracts. You are covered, for example, if the central air-conditioning system peters out during an August heat wave.

While specific plans differ, most warranty companies will repair breakdowns in the electrical, plumbing, heating, and cooling systems and either fix or replace such major appliances as refrigerators, ranges, and dishwashers.

The price of protecting an existing house is $270 to $300 a year. In addition, some companies charge an extra $25 to $50 each time a repairman makes a house call or an appliance is replaced. Other warranties have a $50 to $100 deductible. These costs are rather steep, so you should purchase coverage only on older homes where breakdowns are more likely.

If you are going to buy a home warranty, investigate the financial stability of the company offering it before you write the check. Some programs are underwritten by insurance companies, which means that should the warranty concern go out of business, the insurance company would honor homeowners' claims. And be sure to avoid expensive overlapping coverage by checking whether any warranties you have on appliances or guarantees on recent repairs of major plumbing, electrical, and heating systems are still in effect.

Financing

Checklist
When buying homeowners insurance, remember to:

☐ Insure your home for at least 80 percent of its replacement cost.

☐ Make sure the policy indexes your home's replacement cost to the rate of inflation.

☐ Raise your coverage to reflect increases in the replacement cost of your home because of improvements.

☐ Choose the highest deductible you can comfortably handle.

☐ Insure your home's contents for their replacement cost rather than for their actual cash value.

☐ Purchase at least $100,000 of liability coverage; the $25,000 offered by many policies is inadequate.

☐ Add an incidental business option to your policy if you run a part-time business out of your home.

☐ Take advantage of discounts on premium costs of up to 20 percent for new homes, 5 percent for installing dead bolts and smoke detectors, and 20 percent for sophisticated fire- and burglar-alarm systems.

Your Shelter from Taxes

Richard Eisenberg

> Mortgage interest and property taxes are two of the many deductions your home can generate.

Your house, condominium, or cooperative apartment can shelter you from taxes as well as from the elements. It provides you with deductions when you buy it, while you live in it, and when you sell it.

Congress and the Reagan Administration are serious about tax reform, but you can feel confident that most, if not all, of the present tax deductions for a primary residence will survive. "The American dream is built around the federal tax subsidies for home mortgage interest and local property taxes," says William Offutt, a Washington, D.C., tax partner with the accounting firm Alexander Grant & Co.

Tax breaks for home ownership begin even before you lasso a mortgage. If you must move because of your job, you can write off the cost of the mover, except for amounts that your company reimburses. There's a $3,000 limit on deductions for other move-related expenses, such as traveling costs to find a new house. For you to qualify for these deductions, the distance between your new job and your old residence must be at least 35 miles greater than the distance from your old job to your old residence, and you must be employed full-time for 39 weeks in the year after the move. Self-employed people must work 78 weeks within two years of moving. You can take these write-offs if you haven't met the work test yet but expect to. Use Form 3903, available at local Internal Revenue Service offices.

Points you pay to a lender for a mortgage may be deducted as an interest expense on Schedule A, but only if lenders in your area usually charge them and the fees are competitive with those levied by others. If you pay, say, six points in a locality where two is average, only two points can be deducted. The IRS rarely demands proof of typical fees, but if points where you live are extraordinarily high, get a statement from the lender saying so, in case you're audited. You can't deduct points paid on Veterans Administration and Federal Housing Administration loans, and to claim points on other mortgages, they must be charged as a loan origination fee.

A few settlement costs in buying a home aren't explicitly deductible but may stand up to an audit. For example, Dennis Kamensky, an accountant in Oakland, California, advises his clients to deduct the cost of a professional house inspection as an investment counseling expense on the miscellaneous deduction line of Schedule A. "Your house is, after all, probably the biggest investment you'll make," he says. On the other hand, you can't write off state real estate transfer taxes or the county recorder's taxes paid at closing, nor can you deduct your attorney's fees unless they are incurred as part of a work-related move. But keep a record of all nondeductible settlement costs, because when you sell the house, they can be added to your original purchase price, reducing any taxes owed on the capital gain.

Once you own the house, the interest on your mortgage is likely to furnish your biggest annual tax savings. If you financed the purchase with a 30-year, $100,000 mortgage at 13 percent, your interest deduction in the first year would be roughly $13,000. In the early years of the mortgage, nearly all of each payment would be interest. But if you still own the house after 25 years, you'll be paying more principal than interest, so your deductions will be small.

There is one other useful tax rule about interest. You can't deduct prepaid mortgage interest, but you can claim January mortgage payments paid in December.

Property taxes, which typically equal 1½ percent of a house's appraised value, are fully deductible each year. Condominium owners write off both the real estate taxes on their units and a proportionate share of the taxes paid on the common areas of their buldings. Co-op owners can deduct their allocated portion of the association's property tax bill, unless the co-op leases the land and building. Then there are no property taxes to deduct because the lessor pays them.

You can qualify for tax credits if you make your house more energy-efficient, (see "Saving Energy Still Pays," page 78), but repairs and improvements to your house usually can't be written off. Expenses incurred to maintain a home office are fully deductible, however. What's more, you can depreciate the portion of your house that you use as an office and deduct a prorated share of your homeowners insurance and utility bills. The catch is getting the IRS to believe the office is legitimate. You have to prove that it is used regularly and exclusively for commerce. It must be your primary business location or the place where you meet patients, clients, or customers, to qualify for the deduction.

If your house is robbed or damaged, you may be able to claim a deduction for the uninsured portion of the loss. The unreimbursed amount must exceed 10 percent of your adjusted gross income, and the loss must be sudden, unusual, or unexpected. You can include the cost of hiring an appraiser to assess the damage when calculating whether the loss will meet the 10 percent threshold. The U.S. Tax Court recently ruled that you can deduct a loss even if you choose not to file an insurance claim for fear that doing so would raise your homeowners insurance premiums. Casualty and theft losses are reported on Form 4684, also available from your local IRS office.

When you sell your house, you can deduct any penalty levied by a bank for paying off your mortgage early. But your profit from the sale itself is taxed as a capital gain, which must be reported on both Form 2119 and Schedule D. If you have a long-term gain, 60 percent of the profit escapes taxes. The holding period for long-term gains is six months for homes bought after June 22, 1984 and one year for property acquired earlier. You can reduce your taxable gain by adding to your original purchase price the cost of any improvements you've made and such selling expenses as the real estate agent's commission. Fix-up costs may let you defer your gain too if you buy a cheaper house.

The chances are that you'll be able to defer capital-gains taxes permanently. IRS rules say that a homeowner *must* postpone paying tax on his gain if within two years he buys another house costing at least as much as his old one sold for. There's no limit to the number of times you can buy and sell without paying capital-gains taxes. And if you die before taxes are due on your successive house sales, the accrued gains will never be taxed as income. Don't try to pull a fast one, though. If you intend to sell your home and rent for the rest of your life, pay the taxes. Otherwise, when two years have passed and you can no longer defer the tax on your gain, you will have to file an amended return for the year in which you sold your house and pay the capital-gains tax plus interest.

Anyone aged 55 or older who has lived in the same house for at least three of the past five years can exclude up to $125,000 of his gain from the sale of his or her home. A married couple who own the house jointly can claim this tax break even if only one spouse meets both the age and residency tests. The exclusion is a once-in-a-lifetime gift, so be sure you won't have a larger gain from another house sale in the future. Take your time claiming the exclusion. You have up to three years after you have filed your return to notify the IRS about the exclusion. Should you be so lucky as to have a gain of more than $125,000, you can claim the exclusion and also defer taxes on the excess if you buy another house costing at least $125,000 within two years.

Keep a file labeled HOUSE with your other tax records. It will be your best defense in case of a tax audit. Stuff in copies of the sales contracts for homes you've bought and sold, receipts for any improvements and repairs you've made to them, and records of any energy-saving devices you've installed. Hang on to papers that relate to casualty or theft losses. Preserving receipts and filing additional tax forms may seem like a nuisance, but the resulting tax savings will more than compensate you for the effort.

Financing

Checklist

Your home is a tax-advantaged treasure trove, especially if you keep all documents, receipts, and bills that show what you've spent on it. Among the benefits you can claim:

☐ A deduction for the cost of finding a house if you must move to be near your job.

☐ A deduction for points paid to get a mortgage if they're charged separately as a loan origination fee and if the number of points is average for your area.

☐ A deduction for the interest on your mortgage.

☐ A deduction for property taxes.

☐ A deduction for a home office if it is your primary place of business or if you meet clients there.

☐ A credit for some costs of making your house more energy-efficient.

☐ A deduction for casualty or theft losses if the unreimbursed amount exceeds 10 percent of your adjusted gross income.

☐ A deduction for a mortgage-prepayment penalty.

☐ A deferral of capital-gains taxes on the sale of your house if, within two years, you buy another costing at least as much as the first one.

☐ An exclusion from capital-gains taxes of up to $125,000 from the sale of your house if you are 55 or older.

How Much House Can You Afford?

Most people have a rough sense of what they can spend on a house. But when you are buying your first home, your mental arithmetic may not be very accurate. For example, you can't assume that because you have $20,000 for a down payment you can buy a $100,000 house. If your income can't support payments on an $80,000 mortgage at the going interest rate, lenders will not give you the loan. Usually they figure that if housing costs—mortgage, property taxes, and homeowners insurance—consume more than 28 percent of your annual income, you can't afford the mortgage. In addition, they look at your long-term debts—obligations with 10 or more months to run. Including the mortgage, debt repayment should not exceed 36 percent of your income.

This worksheet is designed to help you compute the most you can spend for a house. First, fill in your assets and liabilities to see how much money you've got for a down payment and closing costs. Then analyze your income and expenses to see how big a mortgage you can carry. The down payment plus the mortgage gives you the price of the house you can afford.

Financing

ASSETS		LIABILITIES	
Cash	$	Installment loans	$ ....
Savings accounts	. . . . . .	Credit-card balances	. . . . . .
Stocks	. . . . . .	Student loans	. . . . . .
Mutual funds	. . . . . .	Other debts	. . . . . .
Bonds	. . . . . .		
Life insurance cash value	. . . . . .		
IRAs	. . . . . .		
Keogh plan	. . . . . .		
Employee savings plans*	. . . . . .		
Pensions*	. . . . . .		
Real estate	. . . . . .		
Other	. . . . . .		
TOTAL	$	**TOTAL**	$ ....

*If you can borrow against them

STEP I	Subtract your total liabilities from your total assets. This is your net worth.	. . . . . .
STEP II	Decide how much of an emergency fund you need. Three to six months' net income is typical.	. . . . . .
STEP III	Subtract that figure from your net worth. This is the money you have for a down payment and closing costs.	. . . . . .

MONTHLY MORTGAGE PAYMENT TABLE (principal and interest—30 years)

Mortgage amount	10%	10½%	11%	11½%	12%	12½%	13%	13½%	14%	14½%	15%
$50,000	$439	$457	$476	$495	$514	$534	$553	$573	$592	$612	$632
55,000	483	503	524	545	566	587	608	630	652	674	695
60,000	527	549	571	594	617	640	664	687	711	735	759
65,000	570	595	619	644	669	694	719	745	770	796	822
70,000	614	640	667	693	720	747	774	802	829	857	885
75,000	658	686	714	743	771	800	830	859	889	918	948
80,000	702	732	762	792	823	854	885	916	948	980	1,012
85,000	746	778	809	842	874	907	940	974	1,007	1,041	1,075
90,000	790	823	857	891	926	961	996	1,031	1,066	1,102	1,138
95,000	834	869	905	941	977	1,014	1,051	1,088	1,126	1,163	1,201
100,000	878	915	952	990	1,029	1,067	1,106	1,145	1,185	1,225	1,264

Financing

STEP IV   Add up your expenses and the estimated operating costs of a new house.   . . . . . .

Subtract them from your total income.   . . . . . .

Add back in what you are paying now for rent and utilities, since that money will be available to you for the new house. The total is the amount you can afford to spend on mortgage payments   . . . . . .

STEP V   Divide this amount by 12 to calculate the monthly payments you can afford.   . . . . . .

STEP VI   Read across the payment table until you find the prevailing interest rate. Next, go down that column to find the figure you arrived at in Step V, or an amount that is within a few dollars of it. Then see what mortgage amount that figure corresponds to.   . . . . . .

STEP VII   Add that figure to the one for the down payment and closing costs you have already calculated in Step III.   . . . . . .

Subtract the closing costs, which are 5 percent to 8 percent of the mortgage amount. The total gives you an idea of the price range in which you should be shopping.   . . . . . .

Financing

ANNUAL INCOME		ANNUAL EXPENSES		COSTS OF NEW HOUSE*	
Gross salary	$	Rent	$	Homeowners insurance	$ ....
Alimony	....	Food	....	Maintenance	....
Child support	....	Alimony	....	Property taxes	....
Interest	....	Child support	....	Utilities (including electricity, heat and telephone)	....
Dividends	....	Clothing	....	Other	....
Other	....	Transportation	....		
		Medical and dental expenses	....		
		Insurance payments Life	....		
		Auto	....		
		Other	....		
		Loan and charge-account payments	....		
		Recreation and entertainment	....		
		Vacations	....		
		Tuition and day care	....		
		Savings	....		
		Tax payments	....		
		Utilities (including telephone)	....		
		Other	....		

TOTAL: $ ....   **TOTAL: $ ....**   **TOTAL: $ ....**

*Consult the appropriate stories in the *Money Guide* for any estimates you need to make.

Remodel? Or Move?

Walter L. Updegrave

> If extra space is all you need,
> consider renovating before you
> think about selling.

Trading in the old homestead and moving to a larger, more expensive spread almost always used to make economic sense. During the 1970s, recalls George Writer, a developer in Denver, "I had buyers who'd live in one of my homes for a few years, sell it, maybe make a $35,000 profit, put $10,000 down on a larger home, then invest the rest or take a vacation." The costs of moving—a 6 percent commission for selling the old house, 5 percent closing costs on the new one, another $1,000 or so to the moving company—were easily absorbed by 12 percent to 14 percent annual appreciation on the house.

Today interest rates hover in double digits while the house slouches along at 3 percent to 4 percent a year. That means you may have to live in your home at least three years before its value will have grown enough to cover the costs of selling and buying a new one. As a result, smart homeowners are carefully weighing the advantages of feathering their present nest against simply flying the coop.

Your first step when you're faced with the improve-or-move dilemma is to figure out exactly what dissatisfies you about your present home. Last year *Professional Builder,* a trade magazine, asked 201 householders why they planned to move within the next six months. The reason given most often was that the current dwelling was just too small. Next was a desire to move to a more prestigious neighborhood. These people were also bothered by homes that required too much maintenance, had old-fashioned kitchens or bathrooms, or weren't energy-efficient.

The solutions to some of these problems are easy. If your family with three children under five suddenly runs out of space when the kids become teenagers, you have to move. You can't remodel yourself into a better neighborhood, either, but you don't have to buy a new house to have a Star Wars kitchen. Unfortunately, most of the choices aren't always that obvious, but there are some guidelines to help you decide whether you need a broker or a builder.

If lack of space is your main gripe, investigate ways to squeeze more out of what you have. "Redesigning existing space is one thing remodeling does best," says Neil Kelly, a remodeling contractor in Portland, Oregon.

The goal of gaining a study or a family room is not necessarily worth the expense and hassle of moving if you can convert attic space into a room for as little as $6,000. Similarly, a $10,000 renovation can combine the tiny kitchen and small, separate dining room popular 30 years ago into the large, open eating-and-meeting area characteristic of today's homes. But don't look to the basement for *Lebensraum*. Because contractors must work around exposed pipes and ducts, finish walls and ceilings, and seal the room against moisture, remodeling the cellar costs about 25 percent more than interior work on other parts of the house. And when you finally do sell, you'll discover that basement rec rooms have gone the way of hula hoops, love-ins, and streaking.

You should also stay put if your only complaint about your abode is its energy consumption. Heating bills that make your monthly mortgage payment seem puny might tempt you to unload your money guzzler and buy a newer, more energy-efficient house. Indeed, home builders ballyhoo the energy-saving superiority of new homes to convince you to do just that. But "almost every older home can be brought up to the thermal standards of a new one," says Mark Hopkins, an analyst with the Alliance to Save Energy, a Washington, D.C. energy conservation lobby group. In most cases, this upgrading can be done for $3,000 to $4,000 by installing extra insulation, fitting an old furnace with a more efficient burner, and weatherstripping and caulking windows. Improving your present house is a much more economical route to lower energy costs than buying a new home.

You'll have to weigh the decision to remodel more carefully if your plans call for an addition. Enlarging an existing house is expensive. Says Joseph Walker, a real estate broker in Atlanta: "Once you start adding on to an older home, you wind up spending more than the extra space would cost if you bought a larger home in the same neighborhood." Construction expenses run between $60 and $100 a square foot—about double the square-foot cost of building a new home.

Local zoning laws may also be a limiting factor in planning an addition. Even if your lot could accommodate a house double your home's present size, zoning regulations sometimes stipulate front, side, and back setback requirements that prevent you from expanding your home to the edge of your property line. The deed to your house may also prohibit certain changes or additions. Stop by your local building department to make sure zoning ordinances won't interfere with your remodeling plans.

Money invested in a renovation that's faithful to the character and style of a period home can bring a substantial return on resale. But there are far more nondescript 1950s-style ranch houses and split-levels with little architectural distinction. You should remodel this type of house only if its market value is well below that of others in the area, or if property values have appreciated so much that you cannot afford a larger place.

This was the situation Rick Sommer, an engineering consultant, and his wife Ann faced four years ago. The couple had paid $85,000 in 1971 for a three-bedroom split-level on seven acres of land in New Canaan, Connecticut. But in 1982, the family of four decided they needed a house with room for an office from which Rick could run his consulting business. They also wanted to stay in New Canaan. When they began house hunting, however, they discovered that a bigger place would cost them at least $500,000. "We decided to remodel," says Rick, "because we thought we'd have a better home for the same or less money." The $150,000 renovation added a sunroom and an office and modernized the kitchen and bathrooms. Says Rick: "Unquestionably we made the right decision."

Another good reason to add on rather than move out is a low-interest-rate mortgage. If you bought your quarters more than six years ago, the chances are you financed them at 10 percent or less. Even if you could come up with a large

Improving

enough down payment on your new home to hold your mortgage to the same size, going from a 10 percent rate to, say, 14
percent will boost your monthly payments by more than a
third. What is likely is that you'd require an even larger mortgage. The increase in your monthly carrying charges when
you go from a $100,000 loan at 10 percent to $120,000 at 14
percent is a jolting 62 percent. If that strains your budget,
you're much better off looking for ways to improve your present home. Overreaching may leave you so strapped that you
are forced to defer maintenance on the house, which, in turn,
will reduce the dwelling's value when you sell it.

If you decide to add on to your house, be sure the cost
doesn't raise the value of your property more than 20 percent
over that of similar homes in the neighborhood. Plowing
more than that into a renovation is risky because you're
unlikely to recover those costs when you sell.

It was just this fear that led Jim Hynes, a product manager
for Heublein Corp., and his wife Jan to sell their house in
Derby, Connecticut, rather than remodel it. When the
Hyneses bought the house for $66,000 in 1981, its three bed-
rooms and one bath were exceptionally spacious for a young
couple without children. The second bedroom became a
guest room and Jan, a freelance designer, turned the third
into a studio. But three years and two children later, the guest
room and office had become children's rooms, and the family needed a second bathroom as well as additional living
space.

They considered sinking $30,000 into a bathroom, family
room, and a basement office. They first checked with a local
real estate agent, however, and discovered that their home
was already at the top of the price range in the neighborhood.
Says Jan: "The house was not worth investing in. We'd never
have got that money back if we sold it." So the couple
accepted an $80,000 offer and used their profits to buy a
much larger, four-bedroom home in Weatogue, Connecticut.

Don't even consider remodeling if the real estate values in
your present neighborhood are stagnant or, worse yet, slip-
ping. In this case, get your equity out while you can. Retriev-
ing the money you spent converting your bungalow into
house beautiful is difficult enough in thriving neighborhoods; it's virtually impossible where values are headed
down.

The decision to stay put or start packing is seldom made

purely on the basis of economics. Emotional needs play a very important role. Many young homeowners who bought small starter houses or attached condominiums because those were all they could afford now yearn for the kind of place they remember growing up in: the single-family house with big shade trees in its own yard surrounded, say, by a white picket fence covered with rambler roses. "People still want the backyard and the privacy that comes with a detached house," says William Apgar, director of the Housing Futures Project at the MIT-Harvard Joint Center for Housing Studies. Remodeling your one-bedroom condo obviously can't make you realize this Andy Hardy version of home—only moving can.

Similarly, if your present house is too commodious and you want less instead of more, you'll have to move. Architects and designers are magicians at pulling extra space out of small or poorly laid-out houses, but they can't make unwanted rooms disappear. You may also be tired of maintaining a large older house. Moving to new digs can eliminate the more nettlesome aspects of home ownership such as faulty and frequently noisy pipes and antiquated wiring.

If you find that the neighborhood—once so perfect for your needs—no longer serves them, you have another reason to start skimming the real estate ads. For example, Robert Morton, marketing director for American Appraisal Associates Inc. in Milwaukee, and his wife Pam love their turn-of-the-century three-story home with ornate trim, fireplaces, and 10-foot ceilings. But they're not in love with the city's schools. Now that the couple's five-year-old son is in first grade, the Mortons have begun looking for homes in suburban Sherwood and White Fish Bay, where they believe the school systems are better. Says Robert wistfully, "What I'd really like to do is keep our home and move it to a lot in the suburbs."

The final consideration in deciding to move or improve might be called the inconvenience factor—that is, which of the alternatives will cause the least havoc and misery in your life. Many people would gladly prefer the packing and unpacking, loading and unloading drudgery of a move to the unbridled chaos that results from a major remodeling project. "It's like living on a construction site," says Rick Sommer. "We couldn't use our kitchen for a month. We washed dishes in the tub. And every day there were decisions that had

Improving

to be made—where does the molding go, how many electrical outlets do we want, where do they go, what pattern of tile goes where?" It's a hearty breed of homeowner who lives through a large renovation and comes out with his nerves in one piece. "When push comes to shove," says William Apgar, "it's easier for people to move." Easier, perhaps, but as many homeowners have discovered in the past few years, possibly not nearly so satisfying.

Checklist

Move if . . .

☐ The cost of remodeling added to your home's present market value would put you 20 percent over the price of comparable houses in your neighborhood.

☐ Property values in your neighborhood have been flat or declining.

☐ You yearn for a detached house with a yard in front and back.

☐ Your present home is too large.

☐ You're tired of bothering with the maintenance and upkeep an older home requires.

☐ You have a low tolerance for living amidst the confusion and debris caused by construction.

Remodel if . . .

☐ Your need for more living space can be met by redesigning and making better use of your existing house.

☐ Your house is not energy-efficient.

☐ You're satisfied with the location of your home.

☐ You own a period house.

☐ You hold a long-term, fixed-rate mortgage at a below-market rate.

☐ Moving to a larger house in a comparable or better neighborhood would seriously strain your budget.

Building Value into Your House

William C. Banks

> When you remodel, you should balance your own needs against those of a potential buyer.

The best reason to undertake a major home renovation project is to improve a place that you like and hope to live in for some time. The urge to remodel can be born along with a child who needs a room of his own. Other times it comes from your bank balance: if your fuel bills are beginning to look as big to you as Canada's gross national product, consider adding more insulation to your house. (For more on making your home energy-efficient, see page 78.)

At some point, however, you are going to sell the old homestead. To recover the money you spent enhancing it, there has to be some compromise between the changes you want and the ones a prospective buyer will be willing to pay for. As a rule, the more a project is tailored to your personal tastes, the less likely it is to appeal to someone else. Says Robert Griffin, a real estate agent in Paducah, Kentucky: "One of the most common misconceptions in real estate is that any improvement you make will increase the value of your property. That's definitely not true."

Before you plan a big project, take a look at what's been done on comparable dwellings nearby. The highest return on improvements comes from bringing your place up to par with others in the neighborhood. But if your house is already in the same price range as the others, make sure you don't add on too much. <u>You're not likely to recover costs that exceed 20 percent of the average value of homes in your neighborhood.</u>

Labor accounts for at least half of the expense of any construction project, so if you are able to do some of the work yourself, you can make larger improvements without overstepping the neighborhood price range. Undertaking labor-intensive chores such as removing old appliances from the kitchen before the workers arrive or knocking down nonbearing walls—partitions that do not support the roof or upper floors—can help you cut hundreds of dollars off the overall cost of construction. But for any complicated job, hire a professional contractor. Hammer scars or protruding nailheads, poorly cut boards, and ill-fitting paneling can turn a well-intentioned project into a detriment when you sell the house. Unless you're extraordinarily gifted with tools, leave all electrical, plumbing, and heavy construction to the experts.

To find out which remodeling projects are most likely to increase the value of a house, *Money Guide* surveyed real estate agents, appraisers, builders, and architects around the country. While construction costs and real estate prices vary from region to region, the prices and estimated recovery values cited are representative averages. In order of their probable return on the money you spend, the most cost-effective renovations are:

▶ An additional bathroom: 80 percent to 125 percent. You are likely to recoup the full cost of a new bathroom if you've got only one to start with; in this case, even a new half-bath—just a toilet and sink—should return every dollar you spend on it. You'll recover the outlay for a third bath if it is the only one on the floor or is added to a bedroom to create privacy. Enlarging the master bath appeals to buyers as well. Expect to pay about $4,500 for a simple loo with a one-person tub. An elaborate *salle de bain* with a sunken tub for two and twin sinks costs $8,000 to $15,000.

Don't skimp on the finishing touches. An elegant ceramic-tile floor ($10 a square foot installed) creates a far better impression on a buyer than vinyl ($5 a square foot). Install bathroom outlets with ground-fault interrupters ($25 each). They are special automatic trip-switch outlets that eliminate the danger of shocks when you're standing on a wet floor using an electric shaver or hair dryer.

▶ Remodeled kitchen: 80 percent to 125 percent. A modern kitchen is both a workplace and family room. As the spot

Improving

where the meals are cooked, it needs new appliances, plenty of storage space, and a step-saving layout that positions stove, refrigerator, and sink close together. As the room where the family congregates, it should also be sunny and spacious enough for an informal eating area. Try to confine your spending to about 10 percent of the estimated value of your house. If you work within the existing kitchen floor space, figure on $5,000 to $10,000 for appliances, cabinets, and a new floor.

▶ Fireplace: 50 percent to 100 percent. No matter what part of the country you live in, laying out $2,500 to $6,500 to put a fireplace in the family or living room is usually worthwhile. Your return will be highest if all the houses near you have fireplaces because bargain hunters will expect to pay less for the one home without a hearth. You should spend an extra $700 or so for glass doors to reduce the flow of warm room air up the chimney and a heat recirculator to blow flame-warmed air back into the room.

▶ Additional room: 40 percent to 75 percent. Although it may seem like the most alluring improvement of all, an addition is almost certain to cost more than it will be worth when you sell. To get the highest possible return on your investment, make sure it harmonizes with the design of your home. You're likely to benefit most from a third bedroom with a bath. But whatever you add, it should not be a one-purpose room. You may want it for entertaining, but a buyer may need the space for a home office. In this case, the money you spent on a wet bar or fancy wiring for your TV, stereo, and VCR is wasted. Plan to pay between $60 and $100 a square foot for a standard 12-foot-by-14-foot addition.

▶ Porch, deck, or patio: 40 percent to 70 percent. Many people are discovering the joys of staying at home. Wood decks covering about 320 square feet cost $2,500 to $5,000, although redwood can run as high as $8,000. For a standard 120-square-foot brick or flagstone patio set on a concrete slab, you'll probably pay $750 to $850.

▶ Attic, basement, or garage conversion: 30 percent to 60 percent. Transforming existing spaces into living areas is usually less expensive than new construction because the walls, foundation, and roof are already in place. However, the return is often correspondingly lower because future owners may not appreciate the change. Thus if you turn the garage into a game room, you eliminate buyers who want a garage. <u>Costs for typical interior conversions run about $30 to $50 a square foot.</u>

▶ Swimming pool or hot tub: 20 percent to 50 percent. Unless you live in a neighborhood where pools are commonplace, you'll probably lose most of the money you sink into one. Buyers look at it and often see only an ocean of maintenance costs and a dangerous temptation for children. The typical 16-foot-by-32-foot in-ground pool costs roughly $12,000. A built-in hot tub, which can run up to $12,000, is also a luxury that has to be paid for by the owner. Unless these heated rain barrels are the neighborhood norm, buyers usually aren't sufficiently impressed by them to redeem more than 30 percent of your cost.

If you plan to move within a few years and you're thinking of pure profit unsullied by personal enjoyment, it's best to resist elaborate remodeling. Stick with a simple extra bathroom or a no-frills kitchen renovation. Says Bryan Patchan, executive director of the Remodelors Council of the National Association of Home Builders: "The hassle of extensive new construction just isn't worth it if you're going to sell in less than three years." Should you plan to remain in the house for at least five years, however, you'll have time to delight in the changes you've wrought and an asset that's in reasonably new condition to sell. Don't fret much about the resale value of your improvements if you hope to stay in your house indefinitely. In this case, the payoff is years of personal enjoyment.

Improving

SAVING ENERGY STILL PAYS

In recent years Americans have learned to conserve energy: today we use 20 percent less per household than we did in 1973, when a barrel of crude oil was cheaper than a pair of movie tickets. But now that fuel prices seem to have leveled off, does it still pay to invest in energy-saving home improvements?

Officials of the Federal National Mortgage Association (Fannie Mae) and the Federal Home Loan Mortgage Corporation (Freddie Mac) certainly think so. They buy mortgages from banks and savings and loans, and they have been urging lenders to ease borrowing guidelines for buyers of energy-efficient houses. They reckon that the less you spend on energy, the more you have for mortgage payments.

Moreover, homeowners can take a direct federal tax credit of as much as $300 for energy-saving equipment they install in 1985.

To figure out how efficient your home is now, call your local utility. For $15 or less, a professional inspector will conduct an energy audit of your house. He will suggest improvements, analyze the pros and cons of keeping, modifying or replacing air-conditioning or heating equipment, and compute the payback period of any investment. The payback period is the time it takes for your energy savings to equal your outlay. This figure helps you decide which improvements are cost-efficient. It would take only six months for a homeowner in Summit, New Jersey, for instance, to recoup the $9 cost of insulating his water heater. On the other hand, installing six thermal windows for $1,173 would pay him back in 23.5 years—far longer than he might stay in his house.

In general, says home energy specialist Edward Minch of Wilmington, Delaware, "People should aim for adequate insulation, high-efficiency heating equipment—regardless of fuel—and a reasonable amount of airtightness." Start with your attic. The poorly insulated house can lose up to 40 percent of its heat through the roof. The R-value of your insulation—that is, its resistance to heat loss—is stamped on the bag; the higher the number the better. In warm climates, R-19 is enough for an attic; for moderate temperatures, your insulation should be R-22 to R-30; and for cold weather, you'll need R-30 to R-38. Insulation runs $150 to $300 for a typical 1,000-square-foot attic, if you do it yourself. And the energy savings will be at least 25 percent of your annual energy bill.

Insulating your basement walls to R-11 for moderate climates and R-19 for cold areas will also cut heat loss significantly. But if you have any wall insulation at all (most houses built in the past 20 years do), don't bother adding more. The savings generally don't justify it.

Heating systems have been greatly improved in the past decade. A high-efficiency retention burner, which regulates the circulation of air and fuel in your furnace, costs about $650, and in northern states it will repay you within three years. If you have a gas furnace, spending $900 for a condensing heat exchanger that recaptures heat escaping up the chimney will save you 25 percent in yearly fuel bills. An electric ignition system that eliminates the pilot light and a damper to seal the flue when the furnace is off cost $450 and decrease your heating toll 15 percent annually. You'll pay $1,800 to $3,000 for an electric heat-pump system, which works well in moderate to warm climates. That's a lot of money, but a pump costs about half as much to run as electric baseboard heat.

You can keep warm air from leaking out doors and windows with caulking and weatherstripping. Both are inexpensive (a caulking gun costs about $2; caulk, $2 to $6 a tube; weatherstripping, $1 to $10 for 25 feet) and easy to install yourself. They can also cut your fuel charges about 15 percent. Storm windows cost about $65 a window, storm doors about $125 each, and together they will cut heat loss by as much as 24 percent. Invest in double- or triple-glazed windows ($200 to $400 apiece installed) only if your present windows need to be replaced.

Both the Alliance to Save Energy (1925 K Street N.W., Washington, D.C. 20006) and the National Appropriate Technology Assistance Service (800-428-2525; 800-428-1718 in Montana) can give you free advice on any energy problems your utility can't solve. But don't talk yourself into something that's false economy. "A fellow down the street burns $600 worth of wood a year," says Ed Minch. "I spend $600 in oil heat, and I don't have to be out there with a chain saw in July."

—*Ava Plakins*

DOING IT YOURSELF

You can save more than half the cost of a remodeling project if you do the work yourself. A number of how-to books will guide you through most tasks step by step. Among them: *Reader's Digest Do It Yourself* ($19) and *The Simon & Schuster Complete Guide to Home Repair and Maintenance* by Bernard Gladstone ($25).

If you have the skills to do a first-class job, you're likely to come out way ahead on the following no-frills projects. The first figure is the estimated total cost of having a professional provide the materials and do the work; the second is the cost of the materials if you do it.

PROJECT	TOTAL COST	MATERIALS ALONE
One-room addition	$12,400	$4,500
Basic kitchen	10,000	3,500
Finished attic	6,500	1,250
Garage conversion	6,350	1,450
Hot tub	6,000	3,000
Deck (320 square feet)	3,800	1,600
Finished basement	3,700	1,450
Standard bathroom	3,600	800
Paneling a room	800	250
Storm window installation (per window)	80	65

Improving

Raise High the Roof Beams

Candace E. Trunzo

Four older homes provide their owners with opportunities to improve on a good thing.

For many homeowners, familiarity breeds contentment. They have developed and come to rely on a network of nearby shops and services. Neighbors have become friends; children have adjusted to schools. The only problem is the house—it no longer fits. The kitchen is raw material for several Erma Bombeck columns, and Paddington Bear's entire wardrobe litters the living room couch. Perhaps it's time to remodel. That's the conclusion that the four couples profiled in this chapter came to. All of them considered moving to larger dwellings before deciding to stay put and make more of the houses they have.

Another thing they all did was to get help from architects or builders. Some used referrals from friends. One couple tapped the local chapter of the American Institute of Architects for names; another engaged a builder whom they found in the Yellow Pages. All the homeowners received detailed cost estimates before the work began. While it was in progress, either husband or wife remained on hand to oversee the job.

Depending on the strength of the housing markets in their areas, these families might—or might not—recoup their expenditures immediately if they had to sell their homes tomorrow. But all of them are confident that the projects they chose and the quality of the execution will net them future financial rewards as well as comfortable living now.

THE HAGLUNDS: RAINDROPS KEPT FALLING ON THEIR HEADS

Melissa and Michael Haglund of Portland, Oregon, wanted to put their children's toys in the attic. "I was tired of tripping over trucks and dolls in the living room," says Melissa, 33, a political consultant. But the attic in their 70-year-old Dutch colonial house was a poorly designed, barely accessible crawl space. So last summer the couple remodeled. A curved staircase now leads from the second-floor hallway to the 225-square-foot third floor, where there is a family room, study, and storage area. While they were at it, they expanded a small second-floor den by 72 square feet to create a master bedroom and bathroom suite. They also built three decks to take better advantage of views of Mount Hood. Total cost of the remodeling: $36,000, including the architect's fee of $3,250.

The Haglunds bought their three-bedroom house for $68,000 in 1979. Because it is located in Portland's Laurelhurst neighborhood, a well-established enclave of gracious older homes, the Haglunds preferred to put their money into remodeling rather than move to a larger house elsewhere.

They saved about $3,000 by doing some of the work themselves. Before construction began last June, they threw what Mike called a "demolition party." Ten friends and family members, fortified with lasagna, wine, and beer, spent a Saturday taking down lath and plaster on the second and third floors and removing the old insulation in the attic. "It was quite a sight to see people knocking stuff out with crowbars," says Mike, 33, a lawyer. He took a week off from work to install the insulation and to prime and paint the interior walls and exterior siding of the addition.

The work was completed in just four months with no cost overruns, a rare occurrence with any construction project. "I tried to stay on top of things," says Melissa. "When we had any questions we went to Roderick Ashley, our architect." In fact, the only mishap was beyond everyone's control. A surprise thunderstorm one night in June before the roof was completed dumped almost half an inch of rain on the second and third floors. The couple was up until 3 a.m. bailing out to prevent serious damage.

THE WARINS: A GRAND SITE FOR SINGING

Not a single note of discord marred the remodeling project commissioned by Deirdre and Oliver Warin four years ago—the addition of a 600-square-foot music room to their 40-year-old stucco house in San Anselmo, just outside San Francisco. In fact, says Oliver Warin, 53, a geologist by profession but an avid amateur pianist: "My only regret is not starting the project sooner."

The couple and their two daughters arrived in California from Australia six years ago when Oliver accepted a job as an exploration manager for Utah International, a mining company. They knew when they bought the four-bedroom house for $280,000 in 1980 that it would have to be remodeled to accommodate Oliver's six-foot Kawai grand piano and a pottery workshop for Deirdre, fortyish.

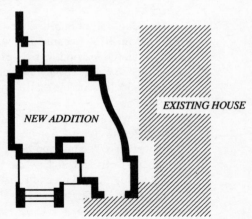

NEW ADDITION

EXISTING HOUSE

In 1982, the Warins auditioned Philip Mathews, a San Francisco architect who was recommended by a friend. The couple wanted something more casual than a formal music room but needed enough space to entertain the friends who drop by for Oliver's recitals or to hear him accompany a young opera singer or a group of chamber musicians. The room also had to be a place where their daughters, accomplished on the flute, piano, and viola, could practice without the sound of music reverberating through the other parts of the house.

Mathews' scheme called for repositioning the main entrance to the house so that the music room would be separated from the rest of the home by a new entry hall. The piano stands in a contoured pit whose shape echoes its curves. Underneath is a four-inch concrete slab covered by a layer of two-by-fours and a layer of five-eighth-inch plywood to soundproof the room. The far wall is also designed in a gentle arc with floor-to-ceiling glassblock panels. Built-in bookshelves behind the piano contain a music library.

The house was valued at $300,000 before the renovation, which also included a six-foot-by-11-foot redwood deck in back. The additions cost $45,000, plus a $5,000 fee for the architect. Although the house was recently appraised at $400,000, Oliver Warin isn't interested in improving its resale value. "If something in your life is really important to you," he says, "you make your home suit it whatever the expense."

THE BENZES: ROOMS FOR WINE AND ROSES

While the Benz family didn't exactly outgrow the modest three-bedroom ranch in Wauwatosa, Wisconsin, they bought 16 years ago, it no longer befit their circumstances. When they moved in—with one babe in arms and another on the way—the $50,000 starter home had all the comforts: a family room, two bathrooms, and even a formal dining room.

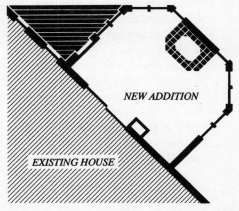

NEW ADDITION

EXISTING HOUSE

Robert Benz, now 45, was just moving up in the family motor oil business. Then as the Benzes' income and children grew, they thought about moving to a more affluent suburb. They even considered a custom-built house. But in 1984 the

Improving

couple and their teenage son and daughter decided to remodel instead so they could remain 10 minutes from downtown Milwaukee and near Lake Michigan, where they sail their 32-foot Islander.

The Benzes spent a total of $75,000 to redo the house, which prior to the renovation had appreciated to $140,000. The most ambitious part of the project was the addition of a 17-foot-by-22-foot garden room that opens onto a backyard ablaze with roses in the summer.

The room was built over a concrete patio that was "useless because of the invasion of mosquitoes in the summer," explains Karen Benz, 40. At first, the couple planned a modest screened porch, but when they discovered a permanent sun room would not cost much more than a porch, they decided to go for the big project and gain a room they could use all year round. The Benzes' architect came up with the idea of a vaulted ceiling to make the room more spacious; their decorator convinced them to put in a woodburning stove, and Karen demanded two skylights so that the kitchen behind the garden room would remain sunny.

The Benzes also turned their unpainted cinder-block-wall basement into a cedar-paneled recreation room for Rob, 16, and Bronwyn, 15, and added a guest bedroom and bath and a cedar closet. At the same time, they converted the basement pantry into a pine-paneled wine cellar and tasting room for Bob's extensive wine collection. "There I was with my best crystal and silver on the dining room table and Bob would be taking guests past the trash in the basement to choose the wine for dinner," says Karen.

The decision to renovate their first-floor bedroom came last. Not surprisingly, the couple discovered that with the other elaborate changes they had planned, the bedroom was no longer in keeping with the rest of the house. So it was enlarged 150 square feet by extending it into the yard, where it is supported by wooden posts. The ceiling was removed, and dramatic skylights and a ceiling fan were installed in the attic space above.

While the Benzes were involved in the yearlong project— "Bob watched practically every nail that went in," says Karen—they left the design and supervision to their architect, William Winters of Junge & Associates. He was recommended by a friend, also an architect. Says Bob: "It comes down to having confidence in the people you work with.

Remodeling's like any other major investment—you have to understand what you're getting into."

THE THIESES: SHE WANTED A ROOM OF HER OWN
Romantic novelist Joyce Thies, who writes many of her books with a neighbor under the single nom de plume of Janet Joyce (*Out of the Shadows*, Silhouette, $1.95), is grateful to the contractors who remodeled her house on three counts: they did a bang-up job, they provided her two kids, 10 and 13, with a place to play so she could write in peace, and they gave her grist for her next novel. "They were a wonderful bunch of intriguing characters," says the novelist, 36. "I can't wait to write about them."

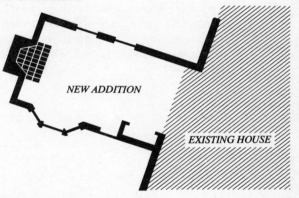

NEW ADDITION

EXISTING HOUSE

She did have talent closer to home to tap: her husband Arnold, 37, is an architect who specializes in commercial projects. But the couple had no time to undertake the renovation themselves, so they sought out a local builder to design and construct the simple addition to their 65-year-old three-bedroom house in Upper Arlington, Ohio, a suburb of Columbus. Joyce called four contractors whose names she found in the Yellow Pages. "They came to the house, but three of them didn't bother to submit bids," she recalls. That left Cardinal Builders, whose vice president, Tom Carskadon, Jr., showed a genuine interest in the project. He submitted a bid specifying exactly what the firm would do for the price. A profile of Cardinal in the local paper reporting that its clients had few complaints about the company clinched Joyce's decision.

Cardinal estimated the job at $30,000, and that's what the Thieses paid to reconstruct the kitchen and to add a 14-foot-by-20-foot family room that opens off it. The new room includes a brick fireplace, a big bay window, and a skylight. The couple's kitchen is open and equipped with a built-in wet bar and oak cabinets. Living with construction was "amazingly easy," says Joyce. "The worst part was when the crew sanded the walls—there was dust all over the place."

Soon after the work was completed in January, 1984, Arnold Thies began staining the oak cabinets, painting the walls, and putting up wallpaper in the family room. His efforts saved the couple only $1,000, but Arnold put his personal mark on the project. Says he: "I enjoy it; it's my therapy."

The Thieses paid $85,000 for the house in 1979. Before the work was completed, the dwelling was appraised at $90,000. If they sold it now, they would break even on the cost of the renovation. But what's more important to them is that Joyce can work on her next novel, *Where Freedom Lies,* undisturbed.

Improving

Making Your Property Bloom

William C. Banks

> Attractive landscaping doesn't
> just grow on trees.

Like a new kitchen or an extra bathroom, trees, shrubs, grass, and flowers can add substantially to the value of your home. Says Torrington, Connecticut, real estate appraiser Thomas Caputi: "A fully landscaped yard with a nice shade tree adds about 10 percent to a home's value, and it helps raise the value of the whole neighborhood." Conversely, Anne Eastwood, a Pasadena, California, real estate appraiser, observes: "Prices can be reduced as much as 3 percent when landscaping is just minimal compared with that of other homes nearby."

Hundreds of species, from Kentucky bluegrass to towering redwood trees, adorn residential property. But before you run down to your local plant nursery, you'll need to know where and how to install your prospective purchases, what they'll cost, how fast they'll grow, and what they'll look like when they mature.

You can get the answers to these questions quickly from a professional landscape architect or an experienced landscape contractor. Landscape architects create a detailed plan of your yard, specifying the types and cost of the plants that are required. Then they find a contractor to do the work. Typically an architect charges a fee equal to 6 percent to 8 percent of the total cost of the job, or about $35 an hour for consultation; for most homes, this means a fee of between $400 and

$1,000 for a complete plan. Add 20 percent to this if you want the landscape architect to find a contractor and oversee the entire job.

A landscape contractor—the person who sells you the plants that the design calls for and puts them in the ground—may offer sound and useful advice for free, but his design training is probably minimal, and he might be inclined to recommend only the species he has in stock. However, if you're adding only one tree or a few shrubs, a contractor may be all you need. For a basic job consisting of shrubbery and two flanking shade trees on a one-quarter-acre lot, he'll charge $1,500. Gardeners should be hired only to maintain vegetation that a contractor has planted. Generally, yard maintenance—not horticulture—is their specialty. Expect to pay them $5 to $20 an hour.

Just as you can design a house by yourself, you can design your own landscape. But if you don't enjoy outdoor work and can't tell a maple from a spruce, you'd be wise to hire professionals. When you do, ask for references and visit some of their previous jobs. Look for a landscape architect who has been in business locally for at least two years, who has a university degree or a license in landscape architecture, and who has been certified by your state landscape board. (Some 40 states require licensing.) It's also a good sign if your candidate is a member of the American Society of Landscape Architects (1733 Connecticut Ave. N .W., Washington, D.C. 20009), a 7,500-member professional association. If you write to them, the ASLA will provide names of members in your area.

A contractor should have at least three years of experience and a reputation for reliability among the nursery owners from whom he buys his plants. He should not only know which species of shrubs are apt to thrive in your yard and the best way to plant them, but also be willing to back up his work with a warranty. Some contractors guarantee the health and well-being of fall and spring plantings for a year, but many assume no responsibility for anything that could happen over a hot, dry summer, when only careful watering by the homeowner will assure the plants' survival.

As with any home improvement, you can spend too much money on landscaping. Most real estate agents and home appraisers suggest that you restrict yourself to no more than about 10 percent of the appraised value of your house.

Whether you hire an architect or do your own plan, it should please the eye and complement the house. For example, many homes have shoulder-high shrubs, such as upright juniper or Japanese holly, of the same girth flanking the front door, low-lying greenery or flower beds along the front wall and nearly identical tall shrubs or trees at the corners. This design creates balance. Rectangular gardens and walks accentuate the vertical and horizontal lines of a house, while rounded shapes and curves soften stark structural edges. Triangular patterns can be used to point toward such desirable features as a magnificent flower garden or a dramatic boulder.

Because different species of plants flourish in different parts of the country, you'll have to rely on local landscape architects, contractors, or nurserymen to find the greenery most suitable for your yard. But the following general guidelines and representative average prices should give you a rough estimate of what your landscaping dollar can buy:

► Trees. Young trees are priced according to their trunk diameters. A two- to two and one-half-inch pin oak sapling, for example, which would be 10 to 12 feet high, costs about $300, including planting. This size gives the most aboveground show for the least cost and is resilient enough to survive planting. The prices of larger trees rise rapidly because a big tree often requires several men and heavy machines to be put safely in the ground. For instance, a cut-leaf Japanese maple only 20 feet tall could cost as much as $2,000.

► Shrubs. These multiple-stem woody plants usually mature in four years and remain vigorous for at least 20 years. Shrubs can be planted in rows to create barriers or accent lines or they may stand alone. Shrubs are judged by their rate of growth, fragrance, and color, as well as the season of their flowerings, whether they are evergreen or deciduous, and the type and amount of any fruit they bear. Generally, slow growers such as azaleas are hardier and easier to maintain than speedier varieties, such as many types of junipers. You pay for species more than size: clumps of foot-tall azaleas sell for less than $2 at many nurseries, but you might have to pay $25 for the same size juniper.

► Grass. All grasses are not green. Some are slightly gray or yellow, and others have red tips. And all are not equally soft, dense, or easy to maintain. Most lawns are grown from seed or from sod. Prices for grass seed range from about $1 a pound for an annual rye grass mix to about $2 a pound for Kentucky bluegrass which is green, not blue. Expect to pay a landscape contractor or a gardener about $3 a square yard to lay down 100 square yards of sod.

► Ground cover. If you dislike mowing grass, you can blanket your yard with one of the 40 or so common ground-cover plants, such as English ivy, pachysandra, and periwinkle. Most ground covers grow four to 16 inches tall and require only faithful watering to thrive. Prices for planting ground cover range from $10 a square yard for periwinkle to about $35 a square yard for pachysandra.

► Flowers. The variety of attractive flowers is so vast that you can establish almost any pattern and color scheme in a garden with $50 worth of seeds and bulbs. Perennials such as daffodils and hyacinths need to be planted just once and they'll bloom every year for about five years. Annuals—for example, marigolds and morning glories—must be planted each spring. Although flowers add a blaze of color to any home, buyers are often more impressed by the size of the garden than by what's in it.

Improving

Checklist

Energetic homeowners can probably tackle any landscaping task that doesn't require earth-moving equipment. But hire a professional to:

☐ Design a major landscaping plan.
☐ Build a retaining wall.
☐ Select all plants that cost more than $25 at a nursery.
☐ Prune branches you can't reach from the ground with a pole saw.
☐ Remove a tree, large rocks, or more than two large shrubs.
☐ Spray insecticides over large areas.
☐ Build masonry walls, walkways, patios, and ponds.
☐ Construct wood fences, large trellises, and arbors.
☐ Plant a bordered garden.

If you enjoy gardening, you can:

☐ Draw your own rough plan, but consult with a landscape specialist before you call in a contractor.
☐ Clear out weeds and unwanted low-lying foliage.
☐ Plant small shrubs and flowers.
☐ Fertilize, hoe, rake, and replant an established garden.
☐ Spray insecticides—downwind—over small areas at ground level.

Hiring the Help You Need

William C. Banks

Paying for expertise from architects, contractors, and decorators can save you money in the long run.

They are the reigning triumvirate of the home improvement industry: the architect designs the house or new addition, the contractor oversees the building of it, and the interior designer furnishes and decorates it. They can prevent you from making costly mistakes and even save you enough money to offset their fees by negotiating better terms for labor and materials than you would get on your own. But if you give them free rein, their fees can jack up the cost of your home improvement 30 percent.

To determine when to hire a specialist, you'll have to know exactly what he can do for you, how much he charges for his work and how you can find one who's both talented and reliable. Even if you succeed, you can't sit back and leave your home in his hands. The most successful and cost-effective remodeling projects are those that are monitored conscientiously by the homeowner.

ARCHITECTS

Architects are trained to design your house on paper from the foundation footings to the chimney cap. They must have bachelor's or master's degrees in architecture from accredited universities, and most graduates spend the five years in apprenticeship with large firms to get experience. Building designers are equally qualified to draw up home remodeling plans; they are also trained in residential design, but they lack a year's courses in the construction of tall buildings. In most states an architect must approve a building designer's plans before a building permit can be issued. Building designers who are not in business for themselves usually work for a construction company or an architectural firm.

Engage an architect or a building designer for major projects—those costing $20,000 and up—that require complex designs, such as a large new wing connected to the house by an enclosed walkway, or extensive structural changes, like the addition of a second story. "Jobs like these are considerable investments," says Paul Heyer, dean of the Pratt Institute's School of Architecture in Brooklyn, New York. "You should hire an architect to make sure your money is well-spent." If your plans are more modest—say, adding a new room on one side of the house—most contractors can provide an adequate plan.

The services you can expect when you hire architects and building designers range from a one-hour house call to discuss your remodeling ideas in general terms to the development of a complete set of plans, including detailed lists of materials, to taking charge of construction. In most cases, however, an architect or building designer will recommend a general contractor to organize and supervise construction. Says New York City architect Richard H. Lewis: "The most common misconception people have is that an architect oversees the work. Legally, that's the general contractor's job in most cases. The architect should keep an eye on things, but he's really an arbiter for any disputes that arise between the homeowner and the contractor."

Fees for architects are established in one of three ways: by the hour, by negotiation for a flat fee, or as a percentage of the total construction costs. If all you need is a consultation and a set of plans, expect to pay $35 to $100 an hour, depending on the difficulty of the job and the architect's opinion of his reputation. It usually takes 50 to 100 hours to draw up plans for a major addition or remodeling job.

Architects who want a flat fee are likely to ask for 15 percent of the total estimated building cost, which includes the general contractor's fee for supervising the project. For tak-

Improving

ing on the entire job—preparing several possible design sketches, final plans, getting bids from contractors, and visiting the job site daily—expect to pay an architect between 10 percent and 20 percent of the total cost of construction. Fees for building designers tend to be more modest, falling into the lower end of the range for architects' fees.

Always try to negotiate the fee. It does not pay to drive a hard bargain, however. A small premium for proven excellence is not a high price. Many architects offset some of their fee by ordering your appliances and furniture for you at wholesale prices, as much as 40 percent less than you would pay for the same items in a store, and charging you only their hourly rate for locating and purchasing the items. Thus a couch that would cost you $5,000 in a store would cost an architect only about $3,000. Even if he or she took eight hours, at $100 an hour, to arrange the purchase, you'd pay only $3,800. Be sure to ask if he offers such discounts before you sign on.

A recommendation from friends who have worked with a good architect is the best way to find one. You can also write to the 46,000-member American Institute of Architects (1735 New York Ave. N.W., Washington, D.C. 20006) for names of members in your area. Full membership is granted only to certified and licensed architects. You can get a list of the building designers in your area by writing to the American Institute of Building Design (1412 19th St., Sacramento, Calif. 95814).

When you interview your candidates, ask for three or four design suggestions for your project: they'll usually rough something out for free. Visit a candidate's recent residential job and ask the homeowner how the work went and how he got along with the architect. Says Beverly Sanchez, a Washington, D.C. architect: "If you interview an architect whose work you love and who has lots of experience and recommendations, but you have no rapport, keep looking."

CONTRACTORS

Hiring a general contractor is the homeowner's responsibility. The contractor assumes complete control of construction, finding subcontractors, such as plumbers and electricians, and making sure that the crews do the job according to the plan. Your contractor can also take care of securing building permits and arranging for inspections and

insurance. And he sees to it that the subcontractors show up on schedule: for example, the framing must be complete before the plumbers arrive, and the plumbing must be inspected before the crew appears to erect the wallboard.

In addition to orchestrating all the details and scheduling, a knowledgeable general contractor can often negotiate lower bids from subcontractors than you would get. He's also likely to know which subcontractors do the best work. Before he submits a bid for your job, the contractor comes to your house to discuss the project you have in mind. The bid typically incorporates a profit margin of between 10 percent and 25 percent of the construction cost. You pay the contractor, and he in turn pays the subcontractors.

Solicit three bids and make sure that your plans specify the quality, type, and even brand names of materials to be used. Says Potomac, Maryland, home inspector Claxton Walker: "If you have a hardwood door in mind, make sure the plan says so in writing. Otherwise, the contractor will bid on the assumption that it's plywood." Don't jump at the least expensive offer, because a low-ball bid can prove more costly than a high one. That's what Mark Blass, aged 41, learned last year when he built a $37,500 addition on his $80,000 house in Allentown, Pennsylvania. "The contractor went bankrupt, and we couldn't find one who would consider doing the work at the original bid," he says. "It took five months to engage another contractor—at nearly $5,000 more. Meanwhile, we lost about $200 because we earned only 12 percent on money we'd borrowed for the project at 15½ percent."

The written estimate you choose often becomes the contract. But before you sign, review it line by line with a lawyer. The contract should include the start-up and completion dates, a clause calling for a continuous work effort, and a payment penalty if the work is not completed on time. Be sure the contract stipulates that when the work is done, the site will be clean, and you'll receive what is called a release of mechanic's lien—written proof that all the subcontractors have been paid in full. In some states, subcontractors who've been shortchanged by the general contractor can sue the homeowner.

The contract should also say that you'll make your payments in stages. Hand over 10 percent when the work starts and 30 percent as each third gets done. Wait about two weeks after completion before paying the final 30 percent; if some-

Improving

thing goes wrong or you don't get the release of mechanic's lien, you'll have some bargaining power.

A competent contractor shouldn't be hard to find. Get personal references from friends, or write to the National Association of Home Builders' National Remodelors Council (15th and M Sts. N.W., Washington D.C. 20005) and the National Association of the Remodeling Industry (1901 N. Moore St., Suite 808, Arlington, Va. 22209) for names of contractors in your area. Try to visit one of the contractor's jobs that is still in progress—preferably on a Friday evening. If the site hasn't been cleaned up, that's the mess you'll have to live with every weekend until your job is complete. Be sure to ask the homeowner what daily living is like during construction.

INTERIOR DESIGNERS

A professional interior designer is not an arbiter of good taste; he or she is an adviser, a problem solver, and a time and money-saving expediter. There are two types of designers: independents and those who work for furniture or department stores. Both kinds are capable of redecorating your entire home.

Consider engaging a decorator if you don't know what you want your new room to look like or if you haven't got the time or patience to take on the job yourself. Professionals can also help remedy problems of tight spaces or oddly shaped areas. Says Gail Adams, president of the American Society of Interior Designers in New York City: "In the long run, a professional should be able to save you money on any project that costs more than $2,000 by helping you get maximum quality as well as utility."

Although anyone can lay claim to the title, a professional interior designer should have a college degree or some credentials. The New York City-based Foundation for Interior Design Education Research recognizes 66 programs. Among the top degree-granting schools are: Parsons School of Design in New York City, Rhode Island School of Design in Providence, and California College of Arts and Crafts in Oakland. The person you choose should provide you with a detailed plan that specifies which styles, models, brands, and colors you've agreed on. The cost estimate should be realistic, but a 10 percent overrun on one or two items is common. "You should refuse to absorb much more than that," says New York City designer Priscilla Ulmann.

Most independent decorators charge an hourly fee that ranges from $35 to $100, or a fixed fee that is usually 25 percent of the cost of the project, or ask for what is known as a purchase or cost-plus agreement. This is a written commitment from you to buy furniture and material at retail prices through the decorator, who buys them at wholesale prices and pockets the difference. An hourly consulting fee is best for small projects, such as rearranging or reupholstering existing furniture and adding one or two new pieces. A decorator usually requires no more than about six hours to come up with sketches of room arrangements and specific recommendations on color, furniture styles, and floor and wall coverings.

When you want to overhaul the house and replace most of the furnishings, a purchase agreement is best. If your designer prefers to charge a flat fee, pay only half up front and the other half when the job is finished.

Should you decide to use a decorator who is employed by a furniture or department store, you'll find that a consultation fee is incorporated into the price of your purchases if you spend more than about $1,000. Part with $5,000 or more and the decorator will visit your house to create a plan for you. You're most likely to find decorators on staff at such posh retailers as Bloomingdale's, Bullocks, and Marshall Field's.

You can collect recommendations of good local decorators from your friends. Sometimes you'll get referrals from retail stores that specialize in home furnishings or from architects and remodeling contractors. For the names of independent designers in your area, you can write to the American Society of Interior Designers (1430 Broadway, New York, N.Y. 10018). Members must have formal training or at least eight years' experience in the trade. The professional association for retail store designers and some independents is the Interior Design Society (405 Merchandise Mart, Chicago, Ill. 60654). It will tell you which stores in your area employ one of their members.

Before you hire a decorator, telephone your candidate to ask about fees and if he charges for a first visit. Before you hang up, find out if the decorator specializes in a particular style or motif; you don't want an Art Deco expert to draw up a plan for your 18th-century farmhouse. To get the most out of a designer, explain what you think you'd like and how much you're prepared to spend. Describe any special requirements, such as durable child- and petproof furniture.

Don't be intimidated. "The first designer I hired just told me what to do," says Richard McGrath, an accountant in Rochester, New York. "If I didn't take his suggestions, he wouldn't do any work. Nine months later I had a pink room and a bill for $150, which I didn't pay. The decorator I'm working with now spends a lot of time figuring out what I want."

Reporter associate: Susan R. Givens

Checklist
Whenever you deal with architects, builders, or decorators, your chances of getting the most for your money increase dramatically if you routinely observe the following precautions:

☐ Look for someone who's been in business locally for three years.

☐ Try to get recommendations from friends.

☐ Find out if your state requires licensing; if so, make sure the person you hire has a valid license.

☐ Check his credit with suppliers, and ask consumer protection agencies if they have logged complaints against your candidate.

☐ Ask what professional organizations he belongs to.

☐ Double-check the quality of his work by looking at jobs he's done that are similar to yours.

☐ Get all agreements in writing.

☐ Make sure your contract specifies the materials to be used, including their type and grade, and the brand names and model numbers.

☐ Have a lawyer review all contracts before you sign.

Year-Round Upkeep for Your Home

William C. Banks

> You get the workout, but the house stays in shape.

Improving

Is there anyone who cannot come up with one good reason to put off home maintenance chores? A baseball game, perhaps. A sale downtown. A broken shoelace. Unfortunately, postponing routine upkeep leads to thousands of dollars in unnecessary repair and energy bills and erodes the resale value of your house. "Most people assume that a house will go on forever," says Ken Austin, president of Housemaster of America Inc., a Bound Brook, New Jersey, home inspection firm. "If they took the same view of their cars, they'd do a lot of walking."

If nature can level mountain ranges, you can bet that water, wind, sunlight, and pests can make short work of almost any man-made structure. Depending on the climate where you live, some problems are more serious than others. For example, in the semiarid Southwest, sun and pests cause the most havoc; everywhere else, water is the main enemy.

If your house is new or located where the weather is benign year-round, an annual checkup will suffice. If temperatures drop below freezing in winter or if your house is more than 10 years old, however, you'll have to sacrifice at least one weekend each season to attend to essential maintenance chores.

You can save money by doing most jobs yourself; hiring a handyman to do them will cost $10 to $20 an hour. But engage professionals for all electrical work and for plumbing jobs that are more complex than replacing a faucet washer. Many tasks, such as repairing faulty shingles, painting, and pruning tree limbs, have to be done only once every few years. Others amount to little more than routine inspections: for instance, checking for leaks beneath sinks.

Begin by patrolling the entire house to see what needs to be done. Then establish priorities: plumbing and electrical problems should be remedied immediately. Next comes sealing any water leaks in the roof and walls, and after that you should look for ways to plug air leaks so you can cut your energy bills. Finally, tackle cleaning and cosmetic tasks.

Start your rounds outdoors with a look at the roof. Remain on the ground and use a pair of binoculars to inspect shingles and flashing, the metal stripping around the base of the chimney and vent pipes and in the valleys of the roof. If you don't mind heights and your roof slopes gently enough to allow you to stand effortlessly, you can reseal minor cracks and gaps in the flashing yourself with about $10 worth of tar or silicone sealant. A roofer will charge about $70 to $100 for the same job.

Replacing deteriorated shingles is hard work. Common asphalt shingles are usually sold in 25-shingle, 50-pound bundles, making it exhausting and dangerous to carry them up a ladder to the roof. Unless you're in good physical condition, hire someone else for the job. Roofers charge about $125 to replace 100 square feet of asphalt shingles and about $2,500 to put a new layer on a 2,000-square-foot roof (most local housing codes will let you have more than one layer). Slate-shingle roofs often last 100 years, which is fortunate because they are difficult to install. Expect to pay a roofer about $25 a shingle to replace broken slates. Also, train your binoculars on your chimney. If bricks or pieces of mortar are missing, a mason will charge you about $250 to mend the damage.

Gutters and downspouts ensure that the thousands of gallons of rainwater that hit your roof each year are channeled away from the house. Water spilling or leaking out of clogged gutters can enter your home's walls under the eaves and damage the siding and framing, or seep in at ground level, flooding the basement. In the fall and again in the early spring, scoop out the leaves and twigs in the gutters and look for mineral granules. They are a sign that your asphalt shingles are losing their surface and will have to be replaced in two or three years. Spray water from a garden hose into the gutters to check their alignment; the water should flow easily to the downspouts and from them to a concrete splashblock or to a drainpipe. If your gutters are broken or severely warped, a professional will charge about $3 a foot to replace them.

During your walk around the house, examine the paint. If it's beginning to peel off in several places, you'll probably need to have the house repainted. Most homes are painted every eight to 10 years, but the trim around the doors and windows requires a fresh coat every three years or so. Painters charge $15 to $30 an hour, and the cost for completely repainting a typical one-story suburban home starts at around $1,700. For about $4,500, the same house could be sheathed in aluminum or vinyl siding, which insulates the walls and requires no maintenance for at least 10 years; after that, the color may begin to fade.

Indoors, go first to the basement. Sniff around the fuse box for a burning smell; it may indicate an overloaded house circuit. Call an electrician immediately. If your panel has circuit breakers, flip them all one at a time. They should snap smartly; if some feel mushy, have an electrician replace them. That will be $35 to $55 for a one-hour house call. You should have ground-fault interrupters (special shockproof outlets) in every room where there's likely to be water on the floor, such as the kitchen and all bathrooms. Push the test button on the outlets to make sure they're in working order. An electrician will charge about $25 each to install these safety outlets if your house is not equipped with them.

Go up to the attic next. Look for dark stains spreading out from rusted nails in the roofing boards; such stains indicate leaks even if the boards are not damp. Try to correlate indoor stains with shingle damage you may have noted earlier. If you found a few bad shingles outside but see no sign of leaks indoors, you can stave off that call to the roofer for a year or so.

Leaks in the plumbing often result in brown water stains on the ceilings and walls. If you see such stains, look for leaks in the exposed plumbing under sinks and examine the grout around bathtub tiles for cracks and gaps. Water splashing down tiles day after day can soak the framing and cause extensive damage. If the tiles look sound and you don't find a pipe leak that you can fix yourself with a quarter-twist of a wrench, you'll have to pay a plumber between $18 and $40 an hour to find and fix the leaking pipe. Don't delay. Water inside the walls and ceilings not only ruins paint and plaster but also rots wood framing and creates a moist haven for termites.

You can cut your energy bills dramatically by reducing the amount of air that flows in and out of the house. Says Jon Sesso, deputy director of the National Center for Appropriate Technology in Butte, Montana: "Most houses exchange all their air up to 20 times a day. That's a lot of heating work that a furnace has to do." Even if your house is well-insulated and has storm windows, you might still be able to knock 15 percent off your heating and cooling bills merely by caulking the windows and putting some weatherstripping around the doors. Hold a lighted candle near the window and door frames; if the flame wobbles, you have an air leak. Invest about $10 in weatherstripping and caulk to fill the cracks.

Keep the equipment that heats and cools your house working at peak efficiency. Spend $40 to have your furnace serviced every year by a professional. You might get a discount if you call him in the summer, when few people are thinking about their furnaces. In the winter, replace a hot-air furnace's filter ($1 each) once a month, and in warm weather wash the air-conditioner filter every six weeks in mild detergent.

Clean the fireplace hardware: grates, andirons, screen, heat recirculator—if you have one—and firebox. Hire a chimney sweep to clean the chimney at least once a year; he'll charge between $40 and $65. Check the attic air vents for birds' nests; blocked vents trap heat in the attic and foster the buildup of damaging moisture.

Rodents are more a health hazard than a threat to your house, but the longer they stay, the more of them there are likely to be, so it's best to call an exterminator at once. Termites, carpenter ants, and many other varieties of wood-boring insects attack the structure of your house directly. Look for a scattering of tiny termite wings around the windows or thin upward-branching mud termite tubes on the inside and outside walls of the foundation. Sawdustlike deposits beneath timbers betray the presence of carpenter ants. National firms such as Terminix International of Memphis, Tennessee, and Atlanta-based Orkin Exterminating charge from $500 to $1,000 to nuke the intruders and about $75 thereafter for annual inspections and treatment. Termite-killing pesticides are toxic, so if you find chemical deposits on the basement floor or anywhere else accessible to children and pets, call the exterminator back for a thorough cleanup. Chemical odors may linger for several days; if they last more than a week, have the exterminator check them out.

Use great care when you evict wasps or other stinging insects. If you do it yourself, zap them first with a fast-kill insect spray that contains a freezing chemical. Never attack a wasp's nest while you're perched on a ladder: your 10-foot fall will only annoy the critters at work under your shirt. Exterminators charge about $70 to rid your house of most insect nests and rodents.

And speaking of unwanted guests, test all home-security devices every time you make your rounds. If you have a burglar alarm system and haven't recently tripped it accidentally, arm it and open a door or window. Warn the neighbors first. Blow out a match about an inch below each smoke detector to sound the alarm briefly.

Finally, accept the fact that you'll be the loser if you neglect maintenance chores for too long. Says home inspector Ken Austin: "It's just human nature to put these things off, but sometimes that $2 expense you ignored becomes a $100 nightmare you can't ignore."

Improving

Checklist
Annual maintenance is easier and more effective when you tend to your quarterly chores according to the season. Some things, however, such as water leaks and electrical problems, you'll have to check for every time you make your rounds. Because weather and pest life cycles vary widely in different areas of the country, adjust this seasonal plan to suit your local conditions.

Spring:
☐ Examine the roof for damaged shingles and flashing as well as the chimney for deteriorated masonry.

☐ Clean gutters and downspouts and check for leaks and warps caused by ice and snow. Make sure that water is being carried away from the house.

☐ Check the paint on the siding and trim. Probe blistered paint and any damp areas with a screwdriver for rot.

☐ Make sure birds or wasps aren't nesting in your attic vents.

☐ Keep an eye out for termite or carpenter ant wings on windowsills and around the foundation; also look for signs of rodents. If you find any pests, call an exterminator.

Summer:
☐ Wash the air-conditioner filters every six weeks.
☐ Examine your deck or patio for wood damage or masonry deterioration.
☐ Check the drainage in your yard. On a rainy day, look for large puddles on the lawn; consult a landscaper if water appears to flow toward your house.

Autumn:
☐ Clean the gutters again and make sure water continues to flow freely out of the downspouts.
☐ Caulk and weatherproof windows and doors.
☐ Hire a chimney sweep to clean your chimney.
☐ Have a professional service clean your furnace.
☐ Empty all outdoor hoses and in-ground sprinkler pipes. Store the hoses indoors.
☐ Prune tree branches that rub against the house; during a storm, they could rip up shingles or damage siding.

Winter:
☐ Knock loose any ice in the gutters with a broom handle.
☐ Change a hot-air furnace's filter every month.
☐ After it snows, look for places on the roof where the snow seems to melt quickly even on cloudy days. This spot-melting usually indicates a heat leak through a gap in the roof insulation.
☐ Hold a lighted candle near window and door frames to make sure your weatherproofing is airtight.

Improving

Borrowing to Better Your Lot

Robert Runde

Since interest rates are down, now is the time to take out a home improvement loan.

When you get serious about an eagerly awaited remodeling project, two questions arise: What will it cost, and where will the money come from? Happily, you are likely to find that loans are readily available, and interest rates are lower than they've been in nearly two years. So now is the right time to be borrowing.

We show the prevailing rates and terms of the four most popular home improvement loans in the table below. Most homeowners prefer second mortgages. "They are the bread and butter of the home improvement business," says Kendall Kelley, vice president for consumer lending at Beneficial Corp. With a second mortgage, you borrow up to 80 percent of your home's appraised value minus the unpaid balance of your first mortgage. But you must have equity in your house to qualify. If, for example, your house was appraised at $100,000 and you had a balance of $60,000 on your first mortgage, you could get $20,000 to remodel your kitchen and add a bathroom, as long as your income was sufficient to handle the monthly payments. Second mortgages cost one to two percentage points more than the going rate for first mortgages, so recently you'd have paid 13 percent to 15 percent for a fixed-rate loan or 12 percent to 14 percent for the far less popular variable-rate version. You can repay your loan over 30 years, although 15 is more common.

As with any loan secured by real estate, you incur closing costs with second mortgages that can amount to several hundred dollars. At Glendale Federal Savings & Loan in southern California, for example, borrowers pay three points, or 3 percent of the amount of a loan, plus $200 for title insurance and $80 for processing. On a $20,000 loan, those charges add up to $880.

Comparison shopping is a must because terms can vary dramatically even at the same lender. American Bank in Portland, Maine, has offered two kinds of second mortgages: a five-year, fixed-rate loan at 15½ percent and a 15-year variable with an initial rate of 14 percent. You'd make higher monthly payments with the fixed rate—$329 vs. $266 on a $20,000 loan. But the adjustable would ultimately cost more since you'd pay interest over a much longer period. And if interest rates climbed, you could pay still more!

Since first mortgages are less expensive than seconds, you might do better by paying off the original mortgage on your house and taking out a new, larger loan. This is known as refinancing, but it makes most sense if you bought your house between 1979 and 1982, when interest rates were at nosebleed levels. Reason: stiff closing costs. For example, if you have a $60,000 loan on your house and want to raise an additional $20,000, you'd need an $80,000 mortgage on which you might pay two points, or $1,600. Two points on a $20,000 second mortgage would be $400. Moreover, you might be charged a prepayment penalty of up to six months' interest if you pay off your first mortgage. For these reasons, refinancing is economical only if it lowers your interest rate by two to three percentage points.

To refinance or take out a second mortgage, you must have not only equity in your house but also steady employment and a good credit record. There can be no liens, defaults, or judgments against you, and you should not have neglected very many credit or loan payments for more than 30 days.

Even if you have no equity and a less than exemplary credit history, you may still be able to get the money you need through the Federal Housing Administration's Title I and 203(k) programs. Anyone who has a home or is buying one can qualify for one of these FHA plans, regardless of his income. If you already own a house, you can borrow up to $17,500 under Title I for improvements. If you are buying a place that needs remodeling, you can borrow $67,500 for both the mortgage and the improvements under 203(k). In certain high-cost cities, such as San Francisco and Washington, D.C., the limit for 203(k) loans is as high as $90,000.

Your loan comes from a conventional lending institution under both programs, but the government insures it. Since the lender has no worry about default, he often charges about half a point less interest than he would for uninsured financing. Moreover, FHA borrowers do not have to pay appraisal or title fees. If you have a steady income and have not defaulted on a previous government loan, you're likely to get the money you've applied for. The only hitch is that you have to phone around to find an institution that participates in these lending programs. Many would rather not bother with the substantial paperwork they entail.

Many affluent borrowers are turning to home-equity lines of credit instead of second mortgages or refinancing. Popularized by Merrill Lynch and other large brokerage firms, home-equity loans are now offered by a growing roster of banks, savings and loans, and even some credit unions. After opening a line of credit equal to 75 percent to 80 percent of the appraised value of your house minus the mortgage, you can use the money for any purpose, not just home improvements. There are no interest charges until you actually borrow some money—which you can do at any time—and then only on what you've used.

The rate, however, is adjustable, varying monthly in line with an index. Merrill Lynch, for example, charges two to two and one-half points more than the prime rate. In March, 1985, the firm's home-equity customers were paying 12½ percent to 13 percent.

Since you are putting your house up as collateral for a home-equity line of credit, you have to pay closing costs. At Wells Fargo Bank in San Francisco, for instance, there is typically a $250 fee for a title search, $150 for an appraisal of your house, a $150 origination fee, a $125 application charge, and a $45 annual membership fee, similar to those assessed by some major credit-card companies. Many lenders also charge one to three points. But by shopping around, you may find a loan with fees as low as $200 to $300, since not every lender charges points, application fees or membership fees.

Lenders screen applicants rigorously. You should have worked at least two years in the same profession and preferably with the same firm and have a lengthy and spotless credit record. Your debts should be manageable, which means that total payments consume less than 40 percent of your income.

The danger of a home-equity loan is that the repayment schedule can be seductively structured. Some lenders charge interest only. Others include part of the principal as well as interest in the minimum monthly payment that they require. If you are paying interest only, you'll need to have the self-discipline to pay off part of the principal as you go along. Otherwise, when your credit line ends, usually in 10 to 15 years, you'll owe the full amount of the loan. If you can't pay the bill, you could lose your house.

Equity loans and second mortgages are convenient ways to borrow large sums, but their fees make them prohibitively expensive for small amounts. Says Gladys Margoni, loan officer at the Community Educators' Credit Union in Rockledge, Florida: "We tell people to forget about a home-equity line of credit if they are borrowing less than $5,000."

The best way to finance a small project is with an unsecured personal loan. Many lenders will let you borrow up to $5,000 solely on their estimate of your ability to repay, and some will go as high as $10,000 for people with especially good credit, employment, and income records. If you are a member of a credit union or can join one, you will probably find the rates lowest there. Some credit unions recently were charging 15 percent to 16 percent for two- to five-year loans. The comparable rate at banks and savings and loans was 17 percent to 18 percent.

Don't overlook your own resources if all you need is $5,000 or so. Corporate thrift plans often let you borrow against your own and the company's contributions, frequently up to one-half of the money you have in the plan. The interest rate can be as low as one percentage point below the prime rate. An even cheaper source of funds is a whole life insurance policy that is at least five years old. You can usually borrow against the cash value at 6 percent to 8 percent.

Reporter associate: Ava Plakins

A BORROWER'S GUIDE TO HOME IMPROVEMENT LOANS

	Second mortgage	Refinancing a mortgage	Home-equity credit line	Unsecured loan
Interest rate				
Fixed	13%-15%	12½%-13½%	—	15%-18%
Variable	12%-14%	9¾%-11¾%	11¾%-13%	—
Costs				
Points	0-3	0-4	0-2	
Appraisal	$65-$150	$100-$300	$125-$150	
Attorney's fee	$50-$400	$150-$500	—	
Title search & insurance	$125-$150	$450-$600	$125-$150	
Filing fees	$6-$15	$6-$50	—	
Credit report	$5-$20	$50	—	$10-$20
Membership	—	—	$35-$45 a year	
Maturity	5-30 years (typical: 15)	15-40 years (typical: 30)	10 years and up	2-5 years
Maximum loan	$200,000	$500,000	$2 million	$10,000
Minimum loan	None	None	$5,000	$500

Improving

Putting Your Best Brick Forward

Kay Williams

> When sprucing up your house
> for sale, put up new screens and
> put out the cat.

To make money, as any businessman knows, you usually have to spend money. This is particularly true with regard to selling your home. It's a rare house hunter who will look past peeling paint and cluttered closets to envision your house as his home. Thus the dollars you sink into sprucing up your castle before you put it on the market can help you command a higher price for it.

Figure on spending at least $300 on enhancing its sales appeal. The Internal Revenue Service considers these repairs expenses that may let you defer the taxable gain on your house when it is sold if you buy a less expensive house within two years. But the costs must be incurred within 90 days before the execution of the sales contract, and the bills have to be paid no later than 30 days after the sale goes through.

To figure out where to put your money, try to look at your home with a skeptical eye, as a prospective buyer might. "When you first move into a house, you notice little things," says Marsha Liebl, assistant director of the National Remodelors Council in Washington, D.C. "The longer you live there, though, the less you notice." For that reason, you may want to ask for an objective critique from a friend or the real estate agent with whom you plan to list the house.

Your home's so-called curb appeal—how it looks from the street—can make or break the sale. Says broker Barbara Jane

Hall, author of *101 Easy Ways to Make Your Home Sell Faster* (Fawcett Columbine, $4.95): "Buyers arrive at your door *wanting* to fall in love with your home." Adds Teague Van Buren, who buys, renovates, and sells residential property in Montgomery, Alabama: "At least 60 percent of houses are sold before the buyer ever gets out of the car." Because that first impression is indelible, Van Buren advises sellers to focus most of their attention on the exterior of the house.

Unless the walls are blistering and peeling so badly that your house appears to have dandruff, you don't need to spring for a major paint job, which could cost as much as $3,000. But paint the trim. "A fellow can have on a $300 suit and crummy shoes, and he looks like a bum. If he's got on a cheap suit and his shoes are shined, he looks like a million dollars," says Robert Gramza of Century 21 Kay Realty in Park Ridge, Illinois.

For $25, the price of a couple of gallons of paint, you can give your house a shoeshine, touching up the window sashes and trim, the front, back, and garage doors and any areas under overhangs that are dirty or mildewed. Pay a decorator a consultation fee of $75 or so to select the shade that best complements your house. If you choose the color yourself, be conservative. You want to sell the house, not retire in it. Save the fuchsia for a hanging basket on the veranda.

You shouldn't have to reshingle the roof, but obvious signs of wear must be attended to. Call in a professional roofer to replace shingles that have torn loose or curled up. Remove leaves and other debris from gutters and downspouts.

Depending on the season, screens or storm windows should be hung and in good condition. Don't forget to wash the windows, inside and out. When the glare of the sun hits dirty panes, you can see the streaks, even from the street. Patch cracks and potholes in your driveway, and remove bikes, skateboards, and roller skates from the path to your door. If the garage is dark and musty, replace the light bulbs and open the doors. Clear out the clutter, or at least neatly stack those shovels, rakes, ladders, and garden hoses.

Next you'll have to tidy up the yard. Keeping the grounds neat will not only enhance your home's appearance but also suggest to buyers that your yard requires little maintenance. If you're showing your house in the spring or summer, start by mowing the lawn, pruning overgrown foliage, and sweeping the walks. Remove dead trees or bushes and replace them with new ones; mature shrubs are expensive, but you can replant ones from the backyard. If you have a pool, fill it and place your patio furniture around it. When autumn comes, rake the leaves; in winter, shovel the sidewalks.

When you've done the dirty work, step across the street, sit on your neighbor's porch, and let your imagination round out your casa's curb appeal. Replace the faded numbers on your door with shiny new brass ones—they'll look pretty and help buyers find your house. Innocuous finishing touches such as a bright red mailbox or tubs of pink geraniums flanking the front door can sometimes do more to evoke a positive feeling about the house from shoppers than any major expenditure. And once the outside of your house is as appealing as you can make it, it's time to venture inside.

"Regardless of the season, tackle spring cleaning," advises broker Barbara Jane Hall. Prospects will poke into every closet, cabinet, and corner; a clean house will sell a lot faster than a dingy one, and usually for more money. If a major top-to-bottom scouring is more than you can handle, hire a professional cleaning service for about $150 a day.

Kitchen and baths must always be immaculate. A rusty sink, a ring around the toilet bowl, or grungy tile will cause prospective owners to fret about the cost of replacing antique plumbing fixtures. Tile and tubs should be regrouted—this can be done professionally for as little as $35 an hour—and any mildew must be scrubbed off. You can usually cure a leaky faucet by replacing the washer. And don't neglect your shower curtain; if it's seen better days, buy a new one. You can always take it with you when you leave. Finally, put out fresh towels and a new bar of soap.

Whether you have a kitchen straight out of *House & Garden* or one where Betty Crocker could have baked her first cake, it must look well-organized and inviting. Wash spattered grease from the walls and around the stove. Clean the oven, the sink, and the refrigerator, and if you have time before your buyer arrives, wash the dishes that have accumulated in your dishwasher—even if they don't constitute a full load. Mop and wax the floors, and don't forget to take out the garbage. Storage space will seem generous if you discard the empty coffee cans you've saved, and the counters will look expansive if you clear them of small appliances and dish-draining racks. For warmth, add bright towels, fresh flowers or plants, and colorful scatter rugs.

If you plan to leave the rugs and carpets behind, they must be in tip-top condition. Have them professionally shampooed (for about 20¢ a square foot) or replace them if the dog and years of wear have taken an unsightly toll. Scrub or paint dirty walls, but don't bother hanging new wallpaper. You're unlikely to recoup the $150 or so it will cost if you do the work yourself to replace the faded paper in a 12-foot-by-12-foot bedroom. Paint the woodwork instead. Clean out the clutter from the closets, attic, and garage and donate it to the Salvation Army or Goodwill. Better yet, earn the money to finance the rest of your sprucing-up project by holding a garage sale.

Because all home buyers are conscious of energy costs, your heating system should at least appear to work well. Wipe the boiler and the area around it to remove soot and oil stains. And don't be stingy with heat or air conditioning when you are showing your house. In winter, crank up the thermostat and light fires in all the fireplaces. When the weather is hot and muggy, make your house a refreshing oasis by running your air conditioner at peak capacity during viewing hours.

No matter how thoroughly you repaint, replant, and regrout, simple details can be the ones that sway the house hunter. Before buyers come to call, warm the oven and put a pot of cinnamon and water inside for the aroma that evokes homemade muffins. Make sure the sounds of Debussy and not Cyndi Lauper come from your stereo. And by all means, turn off the TV.

Banish the children and any animals. They are too distracting. Buyers who hate kids or cats or both will be uncomfortable with them roaming around; buyers who love them may forget to notice the house. Once the prospects have arrived and you've briefly pointed out what you consider to be your home's best features, disappear. Then the agent will be free to commiserate with buyers over your tacky dining room carpet.

If the house goes unsold for several months, you will have to get used to living in a fishbowl and keeping it clean and neat. Every ploy won't pay off, but once the deed is handed over, it really won't matter what worked and what didn't. Take the case of the homeowner who watched his colonial languish on the market for three months before he spent $800 to have painters do the shutters and trim. Within days the house sold. A few weeks later, he drove past the old place and saw the new owners busy at work in the front yard. "You

Selling

know what they were doing?" he laughs. "Painting the shutters."

Reporter associate: Lionel C. Bascom

Checklist

You can best give your house sales appeal if you do the following:

☐ Tidy up the exterior by mowing the lawn, sweeping the sidewalks, and touching up the trim on the house.

☐ Fill your swimming pool if you have one, and put out the patio furniture as soon as spring arrives.

☐ Hold a garage sale to get rid of junk that clutters your closets, attic, basement, and garage.

☐ Scrub tile, toilets, closets, walls, and the kitchen sink.

☐ Clean the furnace, then run it full blast in winter when house hunters arrive. In summer, turn up the air conditioning.

☐ Welcome prospects with inviting baking aromas and fresh flowers.

☐ Stash kids, cats, and dogs out of sight before prospects come to call.

☐ Make yourself scarce; let the agent show the house.

Selling

Out of the Old House and into the New

Eric Schurenberg

One way to keep your balance in this debt-defying act: sell before you buy.

Homeowners are mobile people. In the course of their lifetime, a typical couple will live in three houses. That's a lot of buying and selling—or ideally, selling and buying—for real estate agents are unanimous in urging that when you decide to move, you sell your present house before you buy the new one.

A case in point: Carl and Anita Bergman. In 1979, Carl, 38, was promoted and transferred by his company to Albuquerque, so the Bergmans put their house in suburban Kansas City on the market. They had bought it in 1976 for about $60,000 and decided to ask for $99,000. When the house hadn't sold after eight months, Anita, 36, joined Carl in New Mexico, where the couple bought another house for $82,000. For the next 13 months, the Bergmans carried two homes, laying out $1,400 a month in mortgage payments. "It nearly killed us," says Carl. Finally they found a tenant for the Kansas City house who was willing to rent with an option to buy. Even so, the $490 rent did not cover the $650 mortgage payments.

A year later, the tenant exercised his option to buy, but at $82,000. It had taken the Bergmans two and one-half years to

117

dispose of their house, during which time they wiped out their savings and ran up $7,000 in debts on their credit cards. "I guess we came out all right," says Carl. "We made a profit in the end, but I still haven't recovered from the experience."

No move has to be this bad as long as you take some commonsense precautions. Don't assume that your beloved old house will sell as quickly or dearly as it deserves. Get an appraiser's estimate of its value and ask a real estate agent how rapidly homes in that price range are turning over in your area. If houses stay on the market longer than two months, don't even look for a second home until you have a firm contract of sale on the first. If it is at all possible, continue living in the house while it is on the market. Untenanted houses seldom command their asking prices because they look derelict and give the buyer the impression that the owners are desperate to sell. If no one seems interested in your house, lower your asking price, but don't offer to finance a buyer, unless you feel you have no choice (see accompanying box).

While you are awaiting the sale, investigate the area where you will be moving. Ask the real estate agent who is listing your old house for a reference to an agent in the new area, and read the real estate ads in the new town's Sunday paper to familiarize yourself with prices. Drive around and see what neighborhoods best suit you. But don't look at houses; otherwise you may fall in love with a new one while you are still financially wedded to the old homestead.

When you sell first, you risk having to move out before you've found another house. Try to preclude that possibility in your negotiations with a potential buyer. For example, you might be able to postpone the closing date to give yourself time to find a new place. Be aware, though, that an extended closing period also gives the buyer more time to change *his* mind. A better solution, if your buyer is amenable, is to close the deal as soon as possible but rent your house back from him until you can find another one.

If the buyer cannot accommodate you, resign yourself to renting somewhere else temporarily, preferably near where you plan to buy. Granted, this strategy is burdensome, but renting in or near your future neighborhood will acquaint you with the market and make you a savvier buyer.

Despite your best efforts to rid yourself of your old digs before you buy new ones, you may end up temporarily owning two homes. For example, your seller might insist on a closing date that is earlier than the date you set with your buyer. Your problem then is not carrying costs—a month or two of double mortgages probably won't ruin you—but where to get the down payment for your new house when your equity is still locked up in the old one.

The solution is a bridge, or swing, loan from a commerical or savings bank. This financing is designed to tide you over and typically takes the form of a 30- to 120-day personal loan secured by the equity in the old house or sometimes both houses. Interest rates run about two percentage points above the prime. Before a lender will advance you a bridge loan, he'll usually insist that you have a signed contract of sale on your present home.

The worst situation is to have already bought your new home and be desperate to sell the old one. You could find yourself facing this predicament if, say, you were offered a truly irresistible deal on a house you've always coveted, or your employer insisted that you be relocated by a certain time. If you have to buy first, be sure you have a safety net. "Make that purchase contingent on the sale of your present house," advises Sloan Bashinsky, author of *Selling Your Home Sweet Home* (Simon & Schuster, $12.95). Stipulate in the contract of sale that if you are unable to sell your present house within a specified period, the deal is off.

Unfortunately, a contingency clause will not appeal to the seller, who has nothing to gain by holding his home off the market while you try to sell yours. To make such an offer attractive, you'll probably have to pay a higher price for the house than you would otherwise. If the seller still turns your offer down because of the contingency clause, walk away.

A seller who agrees to your condition is likely to insist on one of his own, called a break, or contingency-release, clause. This provision allows him to accept your offer but still keep his house on the market. Then if he receives a higher price, you typically have up to 72 hours to buy the house. Otherwise, the seller is free to accept the better deal.

Meanwhile, your best source of aid in selling your old house may be a real estate broker who promises to buy it if it fails to sell in a specified period, typically seven months. Many local brokers and a national organization, Electronic Realty Associates, will cut such a deal with you. A broker, however, cannot offer you full market value for the house because he has to build his profit into the price he gives you. The ERA program, for example, guarantees you about 85 percent of the property's appraised value. In practice, commissions will reduce your net proceeds another seven or eight percentage points.

For the most part, brokers' guaranteed-sales plans are simply marketing devices designed to attract your business. Most brokers would strongly prefer not to buy your house, so their warranties typically exclude properties that are hard to move, such as those worth more than $200,000 or less than $30,000, or houses on lots of more than three acres or on busy streets. If you live in one of these houses, you'll just have to work harder to sell, perhaps yielding a little more on the price or terms.

Many companies expect that transferred employees will be at their new locations in less than two months. This is clearly not enough time to sell a house profitably and then buy in an unfamiliar location. Many employers, however, will absorb, or at least share, the costs of selling your present house. About 80 percent of the corporations surveyed by Runzheimer International, a Rochester, Wisconsin-based management consulting firm, engage a specialized relocation company such as Homequity in Wilton, Connecticut, or a large real estate corporation such as Merrill Lynch Realty or Coldwell Banker to assume responsibility for selling your house. The real estate concern gives you a check for your equity, based on an independently appraised market value of the house, and your employer pays all the costs of carrying the property until it sells, plus the commission. If your company does not offer you such a program, try to make some financial assistance a condition of your accepting a transfer.

If you are considering buying your new house from a builder's plans, you should be aware of some special considerations. You can't expect to have a contingency clause to fall back on if your new home is going to be custom-built. No builder wants to be stuck with a house only you will like. So make sure you sell your old house before the closing date for buying the new one. Get the builder to agree to compensate you for any interim housing costs you may incur if you've moved out of your old house and the new one is not finished by the promised date. As annoying as it will be to live like the

Selling

man without a country, it is nowhere near as *angst*-provoking as owning one house too many.

THE LAST RESORT: SELLER FINANCING

If you wanted to sell your house in 1982, you might have had to lend the buyer some of the money. One of every four home sales in 1982 required seller financing. Today, interest rates have declined from their recession peaks by almost a third, but 8 percent of sellers still act as bankers, taking back a first mortgage from the buyer. About 5 percent of sellers take back a smaller second mortgage—that is, the seller lends the buyer the difference between his down payment plus the mortgage he can get from a bank and the selling price of the house. Typically, sellers make loans at rates that are as much as two percentage points below market rates.

But you shouldn't subsidize your buyer unless you can't sell your home any other way. Says Garth Marston, co-author of *Creative Real Estate Financing* (Ronald Press/ John Wiley & Sons, $19.95): "Seller financing is generally not a good idea. Most of us have neither the time nor the skill to manage such an investment successfully, nor the wherewithal to back us up if something goes wrong." Such lending is highly risky because most sellers can't evaluate a borrower's creditworthiness as well as a bank can. Thus there's a greater than usual chance that the buyer will default on his payments to the seller.

If you find that the only way to get a buyer's signature on your sales contract is to take back a mortgage, you should protect yourself against an insolvent purchaser by demanding a down payment in cash of at least 10 percent, and preferably more, of the sales price. Insist also that any buyer provide you with credit references and then check them out. Use a commercial banker's mortgage application form—ask for one at your bank—as a model for the information you'll need on the buyer's creditworthiness.

Get advice from an experienced lawyer about the laws governing mortgage lending in your state—they vary widely—and have him draw up the mortgage contract or deed of trust and the note. Consult with your tax adviser too. Federal tax law requires that anyone who finances the sale of his principal residence must charge at least 9 percent interest on amounts up to $250,000 or be taxed as if the rate were 10 percent.

Should you need your principal before the loan matures, you'll have to sell the mortgage to a mortgage banker or private investor for less than its face value. Investors are not scrambling to bid for seller mortgages, so you can expect to lose about 20 percent of your principal. Says William Segal, whose Bethesda, Maryland, firm buys such loans: "Noteholders should scour the market and get several quotes for comparison. That is the only way to learn what value the market places on your loan today."

You are likely to get a better price for your mortgage if you arrange the loan at the outset through the Federal National Mortgage Association's Home Seller program. Here's how it works: A Fannie Mae-approved lender processes your buyer's application and checks his credit as though the lender were making the loan. The fee for this service is typically about 2.5 percent of the loan amount, usually paid by the buyer. At closing, you can hold the mortgage or the Fannie Mae lender will buy it from you and resell it to the agency.

One such lender is National Pacific Mortgage Corp. of Cerritos, California. In July, 1984, when market interest rates hit 15 percent, a typical seller loan was a 13 percent, $30,000 second mortgage with the principal due in five years. If the seller wanted his principal at closing, National Pacific was ready to pay him $27,612 in cash, a discount of only 8 percent. If he wanted to hold the loan, the mortgage company would service it for him—collecting payments, for example—and charge him an annual fee of .375 percent of the loan. Should second mortgage interest rates drop to, say, 13 percent, National Pacific would buy the loan for its current principal value, less a 1 percent fee to Fannie Mae. Like most Fannie Mae lenders, National Pacific buys only those seller mortgages it has helped draw up. To get the names of lenders in your area that participate in the Home Seller program, write to Fannie Mae at 3900 Wisconsin Ave. N.W., Washington, D.C. 20016.

—Martha J. Mader

Selling

Checklist

Some tips on avoiding the financial burden of carrying two houses at once:

☐ Get professional appraisals of your home's value, and settle on a realistic offering price.

☐ Ask real estate agents how long it will take to sell your house.

☐ Study the real estate ads in the city where you are moving, but don't buy prematurely.

☐ If your employer is transferring you, ask him for help in selling your house. Otherwise, list it with a broker who will guarantee to sell it within seven months or buy it from you.

☐ When you draw up the contract of sale, leave yourself enough time before closing to find another house.

☐ Require the buyer to agree to rent the house back to you after closing if you still haven't found a new home.

☐ Make any contract on a new house contingent on the sale of your present house.

Signing Up with the Right Broker

Kay Williams

Go with a local real estate agency, and don't haggle over the commission.

In your parent's day, a real estate broker worked alone with a desk and a telephone and happily closed up shop to jump in the car and show a house. Today he is more likely to have a staff of several dozen, a big advertising budget, and a fleet of station wagons. But the services he renders remain the same: When you decide to sell your house, he helps you set a realistic asking price, advertises your home, and shows it to prospects. He represents you during the negotiation process with a buyer, and once a deal is struck, he helps the buyer find a mortgage.

There are some 600,000 real estate brokerage firms in the U.S., according to the National Association of Realtors. The traditional one-person shop has joined forces with such national franchises as Century 21, Electronic Realty Associates, Gallery of Homes, Merrill Lynch, and Sears' Coldwell Banker unit.

What matters in selling your house, however, is a knowledgeable local broker who specializes in residential real estate. Says Carolyn Janik, co-author of *All-America's Real Estate Book* (Viking, $29.95): "You want to patronize an agency in the same town—preferably the same side of town—as your house. An agent is far more likely to drop everything and run out to show your home if it's not a half-hour's drive away." Whether the firm you select is a small outfit or a branch of Century 21, be sure that its agents know what schools, stores, and churches are in your vicinity. They should also be well-versed in comparables—what similar houses in your neighborhood have recently sold for. As a seller, you put the price tag on your house, but you should consult with your real estate agent to avoid asking too much or, worse still, too little.

Chances are you will never actually meet the broker who owns the agency; most are too busy administering their businesses to meet clients. But do introduce yourself to the office manager. If the agent who takes your listing fails to turn up any prospects, a manager who knows you will be more likely to find a suitable replacement. The person you will deal with most, however, is the listing agent; he or she—more than 50 percent of agents are women—is licensed to represent the broker. The listing agent will show your house and handle the negotiations when an offer is made.

An agent who works full-time in real estate will usually be more up-to-date on the housing market and will work harder for you than a part-timer will. So too will one who plans to remain a while with the same firm. Ask how long your prospective agent has been in the real estate business and with the agency. If the agent is a greenhorn, keep shopping. And if you are satisfied with the agency but not the agent, ask the office manager to refer you to one with at least a year's experience.

Besides showing your house to prospective buyers, a listing agent will screen them to see if they can qualify for mortgages. In some states, however, agents are bound by law to present all offers, whether or not the would-be buyer qualifies for a loan. Once the sale is imminent, the agent will direct a buyer who doesn't have his own financing to lenders who will provide it. For that reason, your agent should be knowledgeable about the local mortgage market. To make sure that's the case, call several lenders and ask what types of loans they offer, what the income qualifications are for each, and what down payment is required. Then ask the agent those same questions. The answers should come quickly, without any references to notes or tables.

There are three ways to list your house with a broker. An *exclusive right to sell* is the listing that your agent will push for. With it, the broker receives a commission if an offer for the house is accepted at any time during the listing period, regardless of who is responsible for locating the buyer and arranging the sale. If an agent working for another broker finds the buyer, the listing broker splits the commission 50-50 with the selling broker. But if your Aunt Sue offers to buy your house while you are still under contract to a broker, the broker gets the full commission—even if he's never met Aunt Sue. The advantage for you of an exclusive right to sell is that your home is marketed through a multiple-listing service, which gives every agent in town an opportunity to see what's on the market.

An *exclusive agency listing* offers you more freedom. The broker you hire is the only broker who may earn a commission for selling your property during the listing period, but you are free to sell it yourself to any buyer you might find and save the commission. There is a trade-off, though: in some places, your house cannot be registered with the multiple-listing service and thus does not get the widest possible exposure to potential buyers.

An *open listing* gives a broker the right to sell your house, but you have the right to sign contracts with other brokers. You can also sell the property yourself without paying a commission. From a seller's point of view, this arrangement is appealing. But a broker has little incentive to market a house that another broker—or you—could sell out from under him at any moment. Moreover, open listings are never disseminated through multiple-listing services.

Don't be talked into a *net listing*. Under this agreement, the broker's commission amounts to everything above an agreed-upon price for the house. If he were to list your home for $100,000 and sell it for $125,000, the commission would be $25,000, or a fat 20 percent.

The listing contract you do sign is a document that is as legally binding as the contract of sale. Therefore, make sure it contains these particulars: the date, the complete address of the property up for sale, proper identification of everyone who owns an interest in the house, the name of the broker, the price you are asking for the property, the rate of commission, the date you are able to move, and whether you are willing to offer seller financing. In addition, spell out the permanent fixtures such as carpeting and chandeliers that are included in the sale of the house.

W The expiration date of the contract should clearly read "November 11, 1985," not "six months from the date of contract." Some contracts also contain a holdover clause stating that if the property is sold to anyone who first saw it with a real estate agent, whether your listing broker or someone else, your broker will receive his commission. The holdover clause is meant to discourage collusion between buyer and seller, and the standard time limit on such an arrangement is three months. Agree to list with the broker for three months. You can then renew your contract on a month-to-month basis if you are satisfied that the broker has done his best to sell your house during the original listing period.

Once he has the listing, the broker should market your house aggressively. That means advertising it in the Sunday classifieds, including it in pamphlets with photos and descriptions of his listed house, and registering it with the multiple-listing service. Within 24 hours after your place goes on the roster, a so-called listing sheet with a photograph and a detailed description of the house is circulated among all member brokers and agents in your area. An agent from another firm with a potential buyer will call your agent and arrange to show the house. Should the buyer bite, the two agents will split the sales commission.

The broker and his agent will be more motivated to push your house if the commission is the standard 6 percent of the selling price. Although 6 percent may seem high, it's 6 percent of nothing if the broker does not sell your house. He collects only when you do. And once a sale is in progress, you may get him to reduce his cut somewhat if negotiations with a buyer reach an impasse. When the two of you are separated by a few thousand dollars, the broker may agree to accept a smaller commission to get things moving again.

You can go to a so-called discount broker, whose commission is as low as 2 percent to 3 percent, but your house may not sell as fast as with a standard broker. When the listing broker earns a smaller commission, so does the selling broker; and for a split of only 1 percent or so, an agent from another firm will rarely go out of his way to show your property. Avoid fee brokers who agree to represent you for a flat amount—say, $700. All they do is deliver a FOR SALE sign to you, answer phone calls, and book appointments. You'll have to show the house and negotiate the price yourself.

When you get an offer, the agent will perform his most

important function: help you negotiate the sale. Negotiations often fail because the buyers can't really afford the house or one side issues an ultimatum, which leaves the other no choice but to comply or quit. To prevent these breakdowns, listen to your agent's advice; you are paying him to mediate. Says Montgomery, Alabama, broker John Walter Stowers, Jr.: "A skilled real estate agent earns his commission by bringing offers back and making sure the parties don't freeze in the track and halt everything."

After you've reached an agreement on price and you're ready to sell, have a lawyer read the sales contract. The wording of the contract is very important, and spending a few hundred dollars on a lawyer's fee is worthwhile insurance against the possible loss of thousands of dollars becaue you overlooked a key phrase.

The sale is usually contingent on two factors: the buyer's financing and a professional inspection of your home for such flaws as termites or cracks in the foundation. If your house fails its inspection, you may have to lower the price or make repairs to satisfy the buyer. Whatever you must do to keep the deal going, do it. Otherwise your house will become what's known as a B.O.M.—back-on-market—pronounced *bomb*, and for good reason. The second time around, a B.O.M. can be a disaster.

SELLING THE HOUSE YOURSELF

The temptation to sell your home yourself—thereby saving the customary 6 percent commission you'd pay a broker—can be strong. But fewer than 10 percent of sellers do it themselves, and for good reason: to make your sale-by-owner effort a success, you must work as hard as a broker would. In other words, you earn the commission yourself.

First, you have to set a reasonable asking price based on the fair market value of the house. For $150 to $300, a professional appraiser will do it for you. Or you can arrive at your own figure. Read the real estate ads in your newspaper to see what owners are asking for similar houses, then go to the town or county office where real estate documents are registered and check how much houses in your neighborhood have sold for recently. Once you know what buyers have paid for comparable houses, you can put a sales tag on your place.

Next, advertise your house in your newspaper's classified section. To get an idea of what to say, study the ads placed by real estate firms. Spend all your advertising dollars locally. Says Carolyn Janik, co-author of *All-America's Real Estate Book* (Viking, $29.95): "Most successful owner sales are to local residents. So money spent on ads in major newspapers 50 miles or more from your home is usually money wasted." Make up fliers and distribute them in your neighborhood: They will accomplish the same purpose as the agent's multiple-listing sheet. Describe your property in detail; for pointers on what to include, drop by a real estate agency and look at a few of its listing sheets.

Like a real estate agent, you must be sure your buyers can qualify for financing. So survey local lenders as to the loans they offer, the down payments required, and the income needed to qualify for a mortgage. Armed with this information, you can judge whether a buyer meets the bank's standards. Ask the buyer's lawyer to send your attorney a detailed statement of the buyer's finances. If you are willing to offer seller financing or if your mortgage is assumable, let the buyer know.

When you get an offer, don't respond immediately. Sleep on it so that you don't agree to something you will regret later. Have your lawyer draw up the sales contract and ask him to be present at the closing.

You can shortcut all the work by enlisting the help of a real estate consultant, not to be confused with a fee broker, who typically charges $700 or so to help sell your house. For an hourly rate (usually about $35), a consultant will advise you about any aspect of selling by yourself—writing ads, determining the asking price, and handling the closing. Some, such as Bedford Place Properties of Salt Lake City, will even book appointments with buyers for you. But these outfits are few in number and operate primarily west of the Mississippi. Nor are they regulated, so ask for references from former clients before you hire one. Another catch: some consultants are affiliated with large real estate brokers, and they'll try to list your property if it doesn't sell immediately.

An alternative if you aren't moving far is to try to get free help from the real estate agent who is attempting to sell you a new house. He may be willing to offer suggestions about financing, tips on haggling, and even draw up contracts for

Selling

you if he thinks getting rid of the old place will give you the down payment on the new one. But be sure you make it clear to him that you intend to sell your house yourself.

Should you get phone calls from real estate agents who have seen your classified ad or your fliers, let them tour your house. They constitute the pool of listing agents you will draw from if you are unable to make a sale. But—and this is important—never let any agent show your property while you are trying to sell it yourself. If someone who saw it with an agent buys it, you're out a commission.

Refuse to show your house to anyone who will not give you his name, address, and phone number and who won't make an appointment to see the property. Allow buyers to view the house only when there are two or more adults at home. "You've got to be careful," says broker John Walter Stowers, Jr., of Montgomery, Alabama. "You're letting total strangers come into your home, look at your furniture, look at your TVs. They may be burglars casing your house."

Remember, you can always list your property at a moment's notice, and probably should, once you've given peddling it a reasonable try. "After four weeks of going it alone," Carolyn Janik cautions, "call in a broker."

Checklist

The difference between a quick sale and no sale is often the broker. Before you put your house on the market, do the following:

☐ Consider only local brokerage firms that specialize in residential real estate.

☐ Choose an agency with a big advertising budget and access to the multiple-listing service to give your home maximum visibility.

☐ Pay the standard 6 percent sales commission so that agents will be motivated to work hard for you.

☐ Meet the office manager of the brokerage firm you select; he or she can help if you become dissatisfied with the service you are getting.

SELLING

☐ Pick a full-time agent with at least a year's experience and a thorough knowledge of the mortgage market.
☐ Read the listing contract you sign very carefully. It's legally binding.
☐ Sign up with one broker for no more than three months.
☐ Take your agent's advice when you are negotiating the sale.
☐ Have a lawyer read the contract of sale.

Buying Rental Real Estate

Walter L. Updegrave

> Despite low inflation and looming tax reform, you can still profit from property investments.

Real estate is replete with success stories like that of Alex Spanos, 61, owner of the San Diego Chargers football team. Son of a Greek immigrant, Spanos quit his job as a $40-a-week baker's helper in 1951 to start a catering business and invested his profits in real estate. In 1960, he formed his own construction company, began building apartments in Stockton, California, and within 24 years amassed a net worth of more than $150 million. Most real estate investors don't become multimillionaires and owners of National Football League franchises, but they have managed an after-tax return of 8 percent to 13 percent a year from well-chosen, well-managed properties. This yield consists of a modest rental income, an immodest amount of tax shelter, and enough appreciation to keep pace with inflation.

Investment real estate today isn't the stellar performer it was during the '70s boom, however. Low inflation is suppressing the rate of appreciation, and bracket-lowering tax reform is huffing and puffing like the big bad wolf to blow down the shelter benefits (see the box on page 138). Even so, now can still be the right time to invest in rental real estate—especially if you find an owner anxious to sell because of the proposed tax reforms. Says Burt Glazov, executive vice president of JMB Realty Corp., a large real estate syndicator in Chicago: "You're not going to steal a good property, but the tax uncertainties make real estate prices attractive now, vs. other investments."

As a beginner, you should look first into residential real estate. It's a familiar investment to anyone who already owns his own home. Office buildings and shopping centers may have more glamour and offer greater potential for profit, but they are too expensive for most neophytes to buy.

Moreover, there is strong demand for rental housing because current interest rates and prices have shut many consumers out of the single-family home market. The residential vacancy rate—the barometer of the health of the rental market—now stands at a relatively low 6 percent nationwide and is well below that in many cities. Says Kenneth Anderson, research manager of the Institute of Real Estate Management, a trade association: "Demographic data for housing demand suggest that vacancy rates will remain between 4 percent and 6 percent in the near future." For the past three years, increases in apartment rents have outpaced inflation. Concludes Leanne Lachman, co-author of *Emerging Trends in Real Estate,* an annual publication of the Real Estate Research Corp: "We're very bullish on the outlook for rentals."

When you shop for a rental property, look for the largest number of units you can afford. That's likely to be anything from a duplex, or two-family home, to a fourplex to a small building with six units. The more units you have, the larger your rental stream and the lower your operating cost per unit. You also cut the risk that a single vacancy will wipe out your income—a problem you face in renting out a single-family home. If you can't afford a larger property, however, a single home is a way to begin. Individual houses are simpler to buy and finance than are multiunit dwellings, and they're also the easiest to manage and maintain. Your tenants usually pay for most utilities and take care of such routine maintenance as garbage and trash removal, snow shoveling, and cutting the grass.

Real estate developers and brokers often push the benefits of buying vacation homes or condos for investment purposes, but you're better off with properties used as primary residences. "Vacation areas are the first to be hit in a recession and the last to recover," warns Albert J. Lowry, author of the best-selling *How You Can Become Financially Independent by Investing in Real Estate* (Simon & Schuster, $17.95).

Like charity, real estate investing should begin close to home. Says Edward Kelley, a real estate consultant in Palatine, Illinois: "There's no quicker way to fail in this business than to be far away from your property." Confine yourself to neighborhoods within an hour's drive of where you live. You'll be more familiar with the market, cut down on the time spent traveling to and from your dwellings, and be more apt to keep an eye on your investment.

Of course, you'll want to put your money where the rental market is tight—that is, a vacancy rate below 5 percent. Says Leanne Lachman: "The lower the vacancy rate, the faster you can raise rents." San Francisco's 1 percent vacancy rate in 1984 helped push rents up 8 percent over the previous year. (For information on quarterly vacancy rates, write the U.S. Department of Commerce, Census Bureau Housing Division, Washington, D.C. 20233.

Another glimpse of what lies ahead in your area: building permits for single-family homes, condominiums, and apartments. You can see the permits at your county or municipal building department. If permits show that a flood of new homes and apartments are planned by local builders and developers, you may want to hold back even if the vacancy rate is reassuringly tight. National and regional building permit figures are available through the Department of Commerce's Construction Division. Lomas & Nettleton, the nation's largest mortgage banking firm, also provides information on vacancy rates, building permits, mortgage rates, and single-family and multi-family housing starts and completions in its monthly publication, *U.S. Housing Markets* (404 Penobscot Bldg., Detroit, Mich. 48226; $130 a year).

The best rental properties are those that are quietly racking up future profits through appreciation as they generate current income. Last year, prices of single-family homes in the Northeast rose 9 percent; prices were up a ho-hum 3 percent in the South and less than 1 percent in the West and the Midwest. The National Association of Realtors publishes national, regional, and some local home-price data in its monthly report, *Existing Home Sales* report (NAR, Economics and Research Division, 777 14th St. N.W., Washington, D.C. 20005; $48 a year). Rates of appreciation vary considerably from city to city within the same region, so talk to local real estate brokers to pin down the specific rate in your area.

Within that one-hour radius of your home, you should look for a neighborhood that's well-maintained and convenient to shopping and employment centers. Avoid extremes at both ends: you don't want to invest in the best neighborhood in the city because there are fewer potential tenants at higher rent levels and vacancies take longer to fill. The purchase prices will be attractive in skid row sections, but tenants can't afford the rent increases you'll need to refurbish your property and boost its resale value. The area you choose should have a low crime rate and ready access to public transportation and major highways. If your potential tenants are families with school-age children, make sure the local schools have a sound reputation. (For additional information on how to assess a neighborhood and schools, see "The First Step: Picking the Right Location" on page 13.)

Do your buying in an established neighborhood rather than risking your money on a new area where your real estate taxes could soar to pay for new streets, curbs, sidewalks, schools, and other services. To find out if tax hikes or assessments are slated for the near future, ask the municipal or county tax assessor. The town or county clerk should be able to tell you about any existing or planned rent-control laws.

Once you have located a promising rental neighborhood, you should look at the buildings that are for sale. Your criteria as an investor are going to be different from those of a homeowner. You might choose to live in a postmodern creation designed by Michael Graves or Robert A.M. Stern, but you can't assume tenants will share your fondness for witty architecture. Don't wander far from styles that appeal to the broadest range of people, such as colonials, Cape Cods, and ranch homes. Easy maintenance is essential. So even though you like the rough-hewn look of natural wood siding or cedar-shake shingles on your own home, as an investor you may prefer aluminum or vinyl siding.

If you're buying a building with several units, be sure the mix is compatible with your location. An apartment building consisting of studios and one-bedroom flats will attract young singles, but it will probably stand empty in a neighborhood of families and children. Avoid properties where the mix of units is unbalanced—for example, efficiencies and three-bedroom apartments. You'll have to attract two differ-

Investing

ent types of tenants to fill the building, and their needs will inevitably clash.

True bargains are always hard to come by, but you can tilt the odds in your favor by acquiring a neglected building in need of renovation and repair. To locate such properties, ask local lenders about their foreclosures. Check in with the property disposition section of your local Housing and Urban Development Office. HUD sells foreclosed properties through competitive bids, and government-backed financing at favorable terms is usually available. In 1984, HUD unloaded about 33,000 buildings this way and in 1985, sold 35,000. But remember that these goods are for sale precisely because other investors couldn't make a go of them. Don't buy unless you're able to identify the problem that defeated the last owner and can come up with a plan for solving it.

Choose a building that needs a facelift, not major surgery, because you don't want to spend more than 15 percent of the purchase price on repairs. The idea is to improve the appearance with a cosmetic paint job, say, or new carpets and modern appliances so you can raise rents. Says Albert Lowry: "For every dollar I spend on improvements, I expect to get $2 to $5 back in profit at the time of resale."

Before you buy, hire a building inspector for $150 to $300 to check the property from cellar to attic for structural defects and such problems as dry rot or water damage. He will give you a written report on what he finds and estimate the cost of repairs. (For more on how to examine the structure of a dwelling, see "Once Over Thoroughly" on page 19.) Avoid buildings that need major work on the foundation, load-bearing walls or roof, or whose plumbing, electrical, or heating systems require a heavy-duty overhaul.

An extensive renovation can pay off handsomely, though, if a property qualifies for the 25 percent historic rehabilitation tax credit (see accompanying box). The credit applies only to properties used to generate income; they must be certified by the Department of the Interior as historically or architecturally significant, and the renovation must be consistent with the building's historic character.

Three information pamphlets about financing, tax incentives, and renovation are available at $2 each from the National Trust for Historic Preservation (Preservation Shop, 1600 H St. N.W., Washington, D.C. 20006; include $3 for shipping and handling). The trust also recently published

The Whole Preservation Catalogue ($24.95), which covers a wide range of historic preservation topics.

Once you have selected your property, your biggest expense as an owner is likely to be your mortgage (see "Getting the Best Mortgage" on page 32). If you can obtain it from the seller, you'll probably come away with the lowest interest rate and smallest down payment. But unless he's so eager to sell that he's offering financing, you'll probably have to turn to your local bank or savings and loan. Most lenders charge one-half to one point more in interest for a mortgage on an investment property than they do for a loan on the dwelling you plan to live in. They believe that the incentive to keep up your payments is not as great if you don't live in the house. For this reason lenders usually require you to buy private mortgage insurance, which can add a quarter-point to the rate and the origination fee for the loan, and they insist on a down payment of 15 percent to 25 percent instead of the 10 percent to 20 percent they ask for when you buy your own home.

A number of federal, state, and local government programs will help you finance investment properties, often at lower rates and with lower down payments than private lenders require. The Federal Housing Administration's 203(b) program, for instance, insures mortgages up to a maximum of $67,500 for single-family homes and $107,000 for four-unit buildings; the maximums are $90,000 and $142,650 respectively in certain areas with high housing costs. A less frequently used FHA program, 203(k) has the same limits and can be used to purchase and rehabilitate run-down one- to four-family buildings. There are no income restrictions on these plans, but both require a 15 percent down payment. If you live in one unit of a multiunit property, however, your cash outlay is reduced to 3 percent of the first $25,000 of the mortgage and 5 percent of the remainder. The loans are made by FHA-approved banks, savings and loans, and mortgage bankers, and the rates tend to be slightly lower than for conventional mortgages because the FHA insures the loans.

Local HUD offices can give you details on these and other federal loan programs. (For a fact sheet on the 203(b) and 203(k) programs, write to HUD, Office of Single-Family Housing, 451 Seventh St. S.W., Washington, D.C. 20410.) Write your state housing authority for information about state programs, and try your city's department of housing and

Investing

community development to see what might be available locally.

Your other costs as an investor will include insurance, property taxes, maintenance, utilities, and repair. Taxes vary widely according to location, but in general, they will consume 12 percent to 20 percent of gross rental income. You're better off having your tenants pay directly for gas, electricity, water and sewer charges, and heat. But local practice often dictates whether the owner or tenant gets billed. Budget about 10 percent of the rents for maintenance and repair, although you can cut costs by doing minor work yourself.

Ideally, you want a property where the rental income at least covers your cash expenses. To keep income in line with outgo, offer your tenants one-year leases. But if demand in your area is particularly strong, you can rent on a monthly basis, which gives you the opportunity to raise rents frequently. Don't buy a building whose carrying costs are greater than its income unless you can afford to make up the difference until you can raise the rent. Cash losses are deductible from your income tax, but as Albert Lowry puts it: "The idea of buying property to lose money every month is stupid."

There are two traps that you must avoid as assiduously as Florida swampland. First, don't get caught up in the infectious enthusiasm of brokers and real estate salesmen and buy before you adequately analyze a property's investment potential. Allow three to six months to investigate different locations and compare different properties before you invest in one of them. Second, be suspicious of claims about any once-in-a-lifetime deal that will make you a killing. Too often that undervalued property turns out to be a white elephant that has already trampled other investors who had similar delusions of getting rich quick. "Don't be greedy," advises Lowry. "Make a reasonable profit and then move on to another building."

THE TAXABLE CONSEQUENCES

The marriage between the federal government and owners of rental property is going through rocky times. The Treasury Department's proposed tax reforms, which the president has endorsed in principle, would erode the tax advantages that currently add so much appeal to rental real estate as an investment.

The major tax advantages of property investments can be summed up in one word—deductions. When you own rental real estate, your profit doesn't have to come from the rent you charge. You can make money as a result of the tax deductions your property generates. The Internal Revenue Service spells it out clearly: "You may deduct from your gross rental income depreciation, repairs, and certain other expenses."

Owners of rentals can depreciate their property (that is, write off the purchase costs) over 15 to 18 years, depending on when it was bought. You can also depreciate the cost of capital improvements—ones that enhance the value of your property.

Operating expenses can be deducted from your annual income from the property. Among the deductible items: salaries for superintendents, the cost of traveling to inspect your property, interest on the mortgage, real estate taxes, and all maintenance costs, including repairs.

You are better off if you can deduct your costs rather than depreciate them, because you'll recover your money faster. That's why the IRS is strict in its definition of what constitutes a repair vs. what is a capital improvement. The IRS says a repair keeps your property in first-rate operating condition. A repair does not add to the property's value or prolong its life. An improvement adds value. Building an addition or installing new plumbing or wiring are examples of improvements. Explains Joseph Trapani, a real estate attorney at the Research Institute of America in New York City: "Replacing the roof is considered a capital improvement; repairing the roof is a deductible expense." To safeguard your deductions, schedule a repair job and an improvement at separate times, "so that the jobs . . . are not lumped together as an overall improvement program," warns a free IRS booklet, *Your Federal Income Tax*. You can get it by writing to the IRS office where you file your return.

Owners who extensively renovate older buildings that they plan to rent out may qualify for tax credits. Unlike a deduction, a tax credit is a dollar-for-dollar reduction of your tax bill. A credit worth $1,000 decreases your taxes by the same amount. The tax credits range from 15 percent of

Investing

the rehabilitation costs on buildings 30 to 39 years old and 20 percent for those more than 40 years old to 25 percent of the costs of rehabbing historic structures. Historic status must be granted by an appropriate state agency and approved by the U.S. Department of the Interior before you can claim the credit.

If introduced and passed by Congress, the Treasury Department's proposed tax changes would reduce the annual amount by which you can depreciate rental property from the current 5.55 percent of the original cost over 18 years to 3 percent of the cost plus an annual adjustment for inflation for as long as the property is held.

The Treasury proposal would cut the deduction for interest to your net annual investment income plus $10,000 until 1990, when it would be $5,000 plus net income. Since the Treasury plan would also reduce the top tax bracket from 50 percent to 35 percent, the value of deductions that survive would be correspondingly less. Tax credits for rehabilitating historic structures would disappear, as would the special tax treatment of capital gains. The value of your property would be indexed to inflation, and when you sold it, you would pay ordinary income tax on the difference between the selling price and the indexed value.

"The rules are simply going to change," says Kurt Karl, an economist at Wharton Econometrics in Philadelphia. "Owners of rental property will have to change with them or expect to pay significantly higher taxes." However, the Treasury proposals include provisions that reduce the tax on interest earned by banks and other lenders. Karl notes that when lenders' costs go down, so will mortgage interest rates, and over the long run, you will have to pay less to buy property. But the economist believes increased taxes will offset these lower mortgage costs so the cost of owning property will remain about the same.

—*Lionel C. Bascom*

Checklist

If you're thinking of investing in rental real estate, you should:

☐ Consider only property within an hour's drive of your home.

☐ Look for an area with a residential vacancy rate of 5 percent or lower.

☐ Give yourself three to six months to investigate several neighborhoods and compare different buildings, including run-down property that you could spruce up with inexpensive, cosmetic improvements.

☐ Choose a stable, middle-income neighborhood that is convenient to highways, public transportation, shopping, and jobs.

☐ Buy a building with a traditional architectural style and the largest number of units you can afford.

☐ Try to get a mortgage from the seller or through a government program.

☐ Be sure the rental income covers or exceeds the cost of your mortgage, taxes, insurance, and other operating expenses.

☐ Limit your outlay for initial improvements to 15 percent of the purchase price.

☐ Keep maintenance costs down by doing minor repairs yourself.

Investing

The Secret of Every Successful Landlord

Tyler Mathisen

> There are many ways to manage rental properties, but they all come down to picking good tenants.

Put simply, landlording is a business. However, it can be a part-time business, as it is with thousands of Americans who own and rent out one or more houses, condominiums, or apartments. The important thing about it is that "You are selling a service," says Francis Kraemer, a full-time landlord in Washington, D.C. "You have to attend to your tenants' needs. If you're not prepared psychologically for this, landlording is not for you."

If you have only one or two dwellings to rent out, you'll probably discover that, apart from the time-consuming chore of finding acceptable tenants, being a landlord should take only three to six hours a month. Still, there's no getting around the fact that things go wrong in bunches. The refrigerator will freeze your tenant's tomatoes, the storm door will tumble from its hinges, and the furnace will go on the blink all in the same week.

You can keep the midnight phone calls to a minimum, however, if the property you rent out is well-maintained. Appliances should be of high quality and kept in working order, for example, and the furnace should be inspected and cleaned annually. You don't have to provide your tenants with the ultimate living experience, but you will save yourself a lot of headaches if you give them at least a pleasant one.

The real trick to being a successful landlord, notes Doreen Bierbrier, a landlord in northern Virginia, "is choosing good tenants. If you do that, the place manages itself." You can put an advertisement in the paper and screen prospective tenants yourself, or you can hire a real estate agent or a property manager to do it for you. Hiring a manager usually makes economic sense if the property you're renting out is far from your principal residence—a vacation house, say—or if it's an apartment building with a dozen or more units. (For tips on hiring a property manager, see the box on page 146.)

If you decide to find your own tenants, you can save a lot of time and trouble by setting strict standards at the beginning and then asking all prospective renters a few questions over the phone before showing them the premises. You may conclude, for example, that you don't want to rent to families with pets, water beds, or Harley-Davidsons—all legitimate prohibitions. Perhaps you want tenants who can move in within a week, or ones willing to pay the first month's rent plus a security deposit equal to two additional months' rent. Most landlords ask for only one month's rent in advance, plus a security deposit equal to it. But you are within your rights in most states to request a stiffer up-front payment.

The disadvantage of overly strict requirements is that you may disqualify some desirable tenants, and your dwelling could go unrented. Each month that it is vacant costs you about 8 percent of its potential annual rental income—while your money is still going out in mortgage payments and taxes.

Once you've weeded out undesirable tenants over the phone, show promising candidates the dwelling and ask them to fill out detailed applications. You can get samples for free or for a small fee from many real estate agents, apartment house managers, and state apartment associations. *Landlording* by Leigh Robinson (ExPress Publishing, P.O. Box 1639, El Cerrito, Calif. 94530; $15 plus $1 for shipping) also contains some sample application forms. Be sure to request the names of the applicant's employer and supervisor, bank, present landlord, and at least one previous landlord.

The most helpful of these references will almost certainly be the landlord's. Interview the applicant's current landlord and ask whether the candidate has paid the rent on time and has done anything that would keep the landlord from renting to him again. Then ask a previous landlord the same questions. Any discrepancy in the answers calls for further investigation. Interview yet another previous landlord or visit the applicant in his present home to see how he cares for someone else's property.

Be skeptical of too rosy a recommendation from a present landlord. He may want to get rid of a problem tenant. Reject anyone who has had a series of landlords in short succession if he doesn't have an explanation. Such a rolling stone could soon have you hunting for tenants again or, worse, could be a person who does damage to property.

Next make certain the applicant has sufficient income and job security to pay the rent. An employer usually will tell you over the phone how long an employee has been with the firm—anything over six months is a fairly reliable indication of job stability. But extracting any information about income is tougher. Employers usually will confirm only a broad income range over the phone. If you want more detailed information, you may have to ask the candidate to have his employer send you a letter confirming that the applicant earns what he says he does. You may want to disqualify tenants whose gross income isn't at least four times the rent, though in today's high-rent times many landlords set slightly less rigid standards. But don't let the decision rest on income alone. Says landlord Doreen Bierbrier: "People can earn $50,000 a year and never pay their bills."

This is why you should telephone or visit a local retail credit bureau or apartment owners' association. A routine credit check on a potential tenant rarely costs more than $30. You won't want to pay for credit checks on all your applicants, of course. But an investigation of the two or three you favor is well worth the tax-deductible expense.

Before you rule out any prospective tenant, familiarize yourself with local antidiscrimination laws. Many are far more stringent than federal rules, which prohibit discrimination on the grounds of race, color, religion, sex, or national origin. Philadelphia, for instance, forbids discrimination because of children, marital status, sexual preference, age, disability, or occupation. Some cities have housing codes that restrict a landlord's ability to limit the number of people to whom he rents a residence of a given size. As a general rule, you'd be wise to keep the number of renters to one fewer than the total number of rooms in the residence. This way you'll reduce wear and tear on appliances, plumbing, and carpeting.

nce you've settled on a tenant, insist that he sign a lease. You can get samples, for a nominal charge, in stationery stores or from lawyers and real estate agents. Make any amendments you think necessary, then have all the adults who will be living in the dwelling sign the lease. This way you are protected if a couple splits up and the one who signed the lease leaves town.

Before the tenant moves in, make a room-by-room inspection with him. Together, note the condition of the walls, floors, windows, fixtures, and appliances. When the tenant moves out, you'll be able to consult your pretenancy inventory and, if necessary, arrive at a monetary assessment for damages. But don't expect your dwelling to be returned to you in pristine condition. Notes Scott Slesinger, executive vice president of the National Apartment Association, a trade group for rental property owners: "When Avis rents a car, the firm expects it to come back with the ashtrays filled. You've got to plan on absorbing the same kind of wear and tear."

If you have kept your place up, chosen your renters carefully, and got everything in writing, you'll probably never have a knockdown, drag-out contest with a tenant. In fact, Francis Kraemer of Washington, D.C., who became a landlord 20 years ago and now owns more than 135 units, says he has had to evict just two tenants in all that time.

Having to hassle with troublesome tenants and, if it comes to it, evicting them is every landlord's worst nightmare. For one thing, eviction proceedings can be expensive, costing up to $2,000 for court filings and lawyer's fees. This is why you want to exhaust all alternatives short of legal action. Try to talk a tenant who has violated the terms of the lease into quitting your rental unit voluntarily. Point out that if you are forced to evict him, the eviction will be reported to the local property owners' association and he may have trouble renting again in the same region. If nonpayment of rent is the issue, as it is in most evictions, remind the tenant that you will report the case to the local credit bureau, thus tarnishing his credit rating.

If persuasion doesn't work, try bribery. Pay the tenant $100 or so or promise to refund whatever remains of the security deposit if he or she will move out promptly. You are forfeiting money that's rightfully yours, but you are also cutting your losses. In some states, you may be able to step up the pressure by paying $25 or so to a local process-serving agency, such as the sheriff's office, to hand-deliver a type-written notice, prepared and signed by you, demanding that the recalcitrant tenants leave.

The landlord-tenant laws on court-ordered evictions vary greatly from jurisdiction to jurisdiction, but they were written to protect the tenant. Therefore, they often specify elaborate procedures for serving notice, numerous appearances in court, and filings in quadruplicate. Figure on the eviction process consuming at least a couple of months. Meanwhile, make sure you are meeting all your obligations under the lease—and under the landlord-tenant laws. Do not resort to heavyhanded threats, midnight dunning calls, or turning off the water or heat. Not only will you compromise your efforts in court, but also you could provoke a countersuit from your tenant.

Fortunately, only a small number of tenancies end in eviction proceedings. But if you must evict, do not shy away from the task. Successful landlords certainly don't.

COMPANIES THAT WILL MANAGE IT FOR YOU

If your tenants pay the rent ahead of time and you can't recall when you last got an irate phone call about a stopped-up toilet, you might just as well manage your own rental property. But if your tenants are not saints, or landlording is only a part-time career for you, consider hiring a profes-sional to oversee your investment. In exchange for a commission that ranges from 8 percent to 20 percent of the gross annual rental income, a property manager will find tenants, handle their complaints, collect rent, and, if neces-sary, evict deadbeats. He will also pay your mortgage, real estate taxes, and insurance premiums.

To make sure your money is well-spent, you should choose a manager as carefully as you would a tenant. Write the Institute of Real Estate Management, Department of Admissions (430 N. Michigan Ave., Chicago, Ill. 60611) for a directory of its accredited management organizations. They are companies that meet the institute's rigorous stan-dards for length of time in business, insurance coverage, and expertise in supervising rental property.

You should entrust your house only to a company or a

department of a realty firm that is primarily devoted to management. Real estate salesmen often take on the job as a sideline in the hope of earning fat brokerage commissions from the eventual sale of the properties. Warns Joseph Clifford, who started the management department of District-Maryland Realty in Washington 30 years ago: "Brokers who are simply augmenting their income will drop the management duties as soon as a hot sales prospect comes along."

Management companies that are mid-size, overseeing 100 to 300 units, give you personal yet economical service. Ask how many properties the firm handles and how large the staff is. A single manager shouldn't be responsible for more than 60 units. Figure on the manager inspecting your property once a month; if it is vacant, however, ask that he show up once every two weeks.

Stipulate that someone in authority be available at all times in case of tenant emergencies. One of the benefits of hiring a manager is that his familiarity with the work of local contractors will get you cheaper and better maintenance than you could hire yourself. Ask to see the ads the company places describing rentals and inquire about how tenants are selected. Be sure you are comfortable with the selection criteria. Since even the most diligent screening process can fail occasionally, you'll want to find out how the company gets rid of obstreperous tenants or no-pays.

The way a company manages its money and yours is as important as how it handles property and people. Before you engage someone, ask for business references. The contractors a company deals with, for example, can tell you if the bills are paid promptly. In looking after your money, a manager can keep separate accounts for each owner or pool all rents in a single account. The second method is more efficient, but it calls for careful bookkeeping. "It's fine to keep everyone's money in one trust fund," says Barbara Holland of Realty 500—Levy Management in Las Vegas, "but you have to make sure that the company isn't borrowing from one owner to pay another's mortgage." Ask the manager how often the accounts are audited by a certified public accountant and demand that he send you detailed monthly statements on your units.

For protection against crime, find out if company

Investing

employees are bonded or if there is adequate insurance against embezzlement—a policy equal to 10 percent of the annual rents collected is about average.

Susan R. Givens

Checklist

You can improve your chances of success as a landlord if you take the time to do the following:

☐ Decide whether you'd rather manage the property yourself or hire a professional manager for a fee of up to 20 percent of each year's rent.

☐ Attend promptly to your tenants' requests for service or repairs if you decide to manage the property.

☐ Set strict standards for selecting tenants and communicate them to prospective renters.

☐ Draw up a detailed rental application for potential tenants.

☐ Interview each applicant's references, especially those from previous landlords, and verify the candidate's income, job security, and credit worthiness.

☐ Familiarize yourself with local antidiscrimination and landlord tenant laws.

☐ Draw up a legally sound lease and have all adults who will be living in your rental dwelling sign it.

☐ Make a room-by-room pretenancy inspection of your dwelling with your renters and take notes on the condition of the place.

☐ Avoid going to court to evict problem tenants until you have exhausted all other options for getting them to leave.

Investing

Housing Terms
You Should Know

Actual cash value. The replacement cost of an item minus depreciation.

Adjustable-rate mortgage (ARM). A loan with an interest rate that fluctuates according to movements in whatever index it is tied to.

Adjustments. Incidental expenses that show up on the settlement sheet that you sign when you buy or sell a house.

Agent. Someone licensed by the state in which he works to sell real estate through a real estate broker.

Amortization. The payment of a debt, such as a mortgage, in installments that include both interest and principal.

"As is" condition. The seller will make no repairs to the house before settlement.

Assumable loan. An existing mortgage that can be taken over by a buyer, usually on the same terms as those given to the original borrower.

Balloon mortgage. A loan with monthly payments that are too small to retire the debt within the specified term, typically three to five years. The balance must be paid in full when the term expires.

Bearing wall. One that supports a roof or upper story.

Break clause. A special condition in a sales contract that permits the seller to keep his house on the market after the buyer has signed a sales contract with a contingency clause. If another buyer makes an offer, the first buyer has three days to agree to purchase the house.

Bridge loan. A 30- to 120-day loan secured by equity in your house. The proceeds are used to make the down payment on a new house when you haven't yet sold the old one.

Broker. A person who has met state real estate licensing standards and can conduct real estate transactions. Many brokers have their own firms.

Builder warranty. Typically, a one-year protection plan that insures a newly built house against defects in the structure as well as in the plumbing, electrical, heating, and cooling systems.

Building designer. A person who has completed the required courses for a degree in architecture except for a year's study of the construction of buildings more than two stories tall.

Buyer's broker. A real estate agent who represents the buyer for a fee.

Cap. A limit on how much the rate of interest or the monthly mortgage payments can fluctuate during the life of an adjustable-rate mortgage.

Closing. The meeting between buyer and seller at which the property

Lexicon

149

legally changes hands. Closing is also known as settlement.

Closing costs. Expenses—beyond the actual purchase price of a home—that buyers and sellers pay at the closing, or settlement.

Condominium. A housing unit in which each owner has title to his own living space and shares possession with other residents of such common areas as lawns and tennis courts.

Contingency clause. A condition upon which the execution of a sales contract depends. Examples: a financing contingency means the sale depends on the buyer's obtaining a mortgage; a purchase contingency means the sale depends on the buyer's selling his old house.

Co-op. A property, such as an apartment, whose title is held by a corporation. Residents own shares in the corporation that entitle them to occupy a certain amount of living space.

Discount broker. A real estate broker who works for a commission lower than the standard 6 percent of the selling price—usually 2 percent to 3 percent.

Double-glazed window. An insulating window with two panes of glass separated by an air space. Also called a thermal window.

Down payment. The 5 percent to 20 percent of the purchase price of a house that the buyer must put up in cash before a lender will give him a mortgage for the rest.

Eave. The part of the roof that projects out over an exterior wall.

Electrical outlet analyzer. A device that when plugged into an outlet reveals improper or dangerous wiring.

Endorsement. A rider attached to a standard insurance policy that modifies the terms of the contract.

Equity. The market value of your property minus the mortgage and any other liens against it.

Escrow. The custody of money or contracts by a neutral third party until specified conditions are met.

Exclusive agency listing. The designation of a broker to sell your house while you retain the right to sell it yourself; if you do, you don't owe the broker a commission.

Exclusive right to sell. The designation of a broker as the only person who can sell your house. If you sell it, you still owe the broker commission.

Fair market value. The price that would very likely be negotiated between a willing buyer and seller.

FHA mortgage. A loan insured by the Federal Housing Administration that requires only a 5 percent down payment.

Fixed-rate mortgage. A loan with an interest rate and monthly payments that do not vary during its life.

Flashing. Metal strips that seal joints in roof valleys and at the bases of roof vents and chimneys.

Footing. A concrete base under the foundation wall that is deep enough and thick enough to inhibit settling.

Gables. Triangles formed by two sloping roof ends.

General contractor. A builder who oversees a renovation or the construction of a house or an addition.

Grading. The slope of the land around the foundation; proper grading causes water to flow away from the house.

Ground-fault interrupter. A supersensitive circuit breaker usually used in electrical outlets. A GFI prevents shocks by automatically cutting the current to appliances whenever there's a potentially dangerous leakage of electricity.

Gutters. Metal or fiberglass channels along the eaves that direct water from the roof into the downspouts.

Half-bath. A small room containing a toilet and sink but no tub or shower.

Handyman's special. A house usually sold in "as is" condition that needs a lot of fixing up.

Holdover clause. A standard part of a

contract with a real estate agent ensuring that even after the contract has expired, he will receive the full commission if someone to whom he has shown the house later tries to buy it directly from the owner.

Home inspector. A trained professional who evaluates the structural soundness of a house, recommends repairs, and estimates their cost.

Homeowner's warranty. A 10-year guarantee that covers major structural flaws in a new house.

Joists. Beams that support the floors of a house.

Landscape architect. A college graduate who has completed four to seven years of study in landscape architecture and who creates a detailed plan of the yard, specifying the shrubs and trees that are required.

Landscape contractor. The person who sells you the foliage the design calls for and plants it.

Lease-option agreement. An arrangement by which you rent a house with an option to buy at the end of a specific period of time at an agreed-upon price.

Lien. A claim against a property by creditors that ususally must be settled before you can take title.

Loan application fee. A lender's charge, ranging from $75 to $300, that you must pay when you apply for a mortgage.

Loan origination fee. One to four points charged by lenders to cover their costs in processing your mortgage.

Maintenance. A monthly fee paid by condo and co-op owners for the upkeep of common areas.

Mobile home. A factory-built dwelling, sometimes on wheels, that is towed to a lot and placed on a foundation.

Modular home. A house that is shipped from the factory as individual rooms or groups of rooms that are clamped together or stacked at the building site.

Mortgage insurance. A policy that insures the lender if a borrower defaults.

Multiple listing. A network (usually computerized) that gives an agent a complete rundown of all the houses listed for sale with brokers in the area.

Negative amortization. The month-by-month conversion of unpaid mortgage interest into additional loan principal so that the amount of the loan keeps growing with each payment instead of diminishing.

Net listing. A sales agreement in which the real estate agent's commission consists of the proceeds above an agreed-upon sales price for the house.

Open listing. The designation of a broker to sell your house, while allowing any broker who finds a buyer to earn the full commission. Or you can sell it yourself and owe no commission.

Panelized home. A home made from wall, roof, and floor panels that are shipped from the factory and fastened together at the site. Such a home is also known as a prefabricated house.

Points. Fees charged by lenders and that are expressed as a percentage of the mortgage amount. One point equals 1 percent of the mortgage.

Precut home. A house whose two-by-fours and other basic components are cut in a factory and shipped to the site for assembly.

Prepayment penalty. A fee, typically six months' worth of interest, charged by some lenders when a borrower pays off a mortgage ahead of schedule.

R-value. The degree to which a material, such as insulation, can retain heat. The higher the R-value, the more efficient your insulation.

Realtor. A member of the National Association of Realtors; usually—but not always—a real estate broker agent.

Release of mechanic's lien. A general contractor's guarantee that all the subcontractors who worked on the project

Lexicon

have been paid in full. Without the release, title to the house is not clear and in some cases cannot be transferred.

Replacement cost. The price of a new item substituted for a damaged one.

Settlement. See Closing.

Stick-built house. One built board by board from the ground up at the site.

Studs. Vertical wood timbers in walls. The builder's phrase "16 inches on center" refers to the distance between the centers of the studs.

Subcontractor. A specialist such as a plumber or a roofer who is hired by a general contractor to perform a specific task on a construction job.

Survey. A measurement of a parcel of land to be sure the house is properly situated within the boundaries. Most lenders insist on a survey before they grant a mortgage.

Sweat equity. The value added to your property by your own labor.

Teaser. An exceptionally low come-on interest rate for an initial period—typically six months or a year—of an adjustable-rate loan.

Third-party service. An arrangement by which a separate company contracts with your employer to buy the equity in your home when you are transferred to a new location. The third party then sells the house for you.

Title. Evidence of ownership.

Title insurance. A policy that protects the lender who had granted a mortgage on a house, if there is a dispute about its title.

Title search. The process of proving that the seller can transfer the title free and clear of liens and other encumbrances.

Townhouse. A dwelling that has its own entrance but shares at least one exterior wall with a neighbor.

Transfer tax. A state, city, or county sales tax on the house that the buyer, seller, or both must pay at settlement.

VA mortgage. A loan guaranteed by the Veterans Administration that allows an eligible veteran to buy a house without making a down payment.